the Hummingbird
REVIEW

THE HUMMINGBIRD REVIEW

SPRING-SUMMER 2017

The Hummingbird Review presents fine writing by contributors ranging from new poets and essayists to fully established literary figures. We are committed to portraying the beauty, culture and challenges of the human experience through literature and art, and cross-cultural writing in all forms.

Published by RI Publishing, Laguna Woods, CA USA
Printed in the United States of America

© 2017 Charles Redner
ISBN: 978-0-9964277-3-9

Publisher: Charles Redner
Editor: Robert Yehling
Guest Editor/Curator: Peggy P. Edwards

Cover design: Terry Houseworth
Interior design: Miranda McPhee

Permissions:

www.hummingbirdreview.com

MARTÍN ESPADA

THE REPUBLIC OF POETRY

For Chile

In the republic of poetry,
a train full of poets
rolls south in the rain
as plum trees rock
and horses kick the air,
and village bands
parade down the aisle
with trumpets, with bowler hats,
followed by the president
of the republic,
shaking every hand.

In the republic of poetry,
monks print verses about the night
on boxes of monastery chocolate,
kitchens in restaurants
use odes for recipes
from eel to artichoke,
and poets eat for free.

In the republic of poetry,
poets read to the baboons
at the zoo, and all the primates,
poets and baboons alike, scream for joy.

In the republic of poetry,
poets rent a helicopter
to bombard the national palace
with poems on bookmarks,
and everyone in the courtyard

rushes to grab a poem
fluttering from the sky,
blinded by weeping.

In the republic of poetry,
the guard at the airport
will not allow you to leave the country
until you declaim a poem for her
                        and she says *Ah! Beautiful.*

CONTENTS
Spring/Summer 2017

PUBLISHER'S CORNER

Gloriaficar las Plabaras – Sing Praise for the Words

In 2006, an author mentioned to writer friends that he'd like to be a part of a literary anthology. With that simple suggestion, and under the guidance of our first managing editor, Kathryn Kopple, *The Hummingbird Review* took flight the following year. For our seventh issue, we finally pay tribute to our inspiration – Tijuana-born, distinguished professor, award-winning author and doer of good deeds, Luis Alberto Urrea.

Full disclosure: the Hispanic spirit had captured me long before I met Urrea. Amid the Philadelphia suburbs where I lived, a remarkable, thriving Hispanic culture flourished weekly – usually on a Friday night – in the form of a party at someone's home. In one room, the flamencos wildly danced, while in another, the mariachis sang. On the porch, Cubanos smoked cigars and talked of politics. Salsa could he heard on the back patio. A Columbian trio strummed guitars and roamed throughout the premises. For years I soaked up this atmosphere, then hitched up the wagon and moved to the Old Pueblo, a sixty-minute ride north of the border where I first encountered Urrea.

For starters, Urrea gives us his thoughts on writing *Into the Beautiful North* and we tease you with the first four chapters. It begins: "The bandidos came to the village…" Immediately, I think of *The Magnificent Seven* and Eli Wallach snarling at the peasants.

We move onto our bilingual presentation of key Latin and Spanish voices over the past centuries. We are eternally thankful for the poems we discovered at *poesiabreve.com.* The English translations come from our Latina editor, Mexico City-born Peggy Edwards. A major shout-out: Peggy, we love you, and this issue does not happen without your intensive labor.

Professor Dean Nelson gives us a window into the mind of former Mexican president, Vicente Fox. Nelson spent time at Centro Fox; we invite you to enjoy a conversation with the former president and Nelson's insight into the man. We are thankful the interview took place before our November elections, least we need "bleep" the many expletives Fox has uttered since.

Yes, there is more: Again, the resplendent, Martín Espada gifts us a frontispiece poem, "The Republic of Poetry."

I toss in one of my many Mexican experiences through "View from My Mexican Cell," while Robert Gleaves delivers "Neruda & Lorca: A Meeting of Poetic Minds." We also hear from the fine Southern California writer Isaac Lomeli, who shares from his forthcoming book, *The Unexamined Life of a Brown Man.*

For our poetry aficionados, we include an evening with former Poet Laureate of the United States Robert Pinsky, as well as the latest poetic suite from John Rouleau — whose verse has graced every edition of *The Hummingbird Review.*

As always, we combine works of students and up-and-coming writers next to those of poet laureates and authors of fame. We remain faithful to our mission statement:

The Hummingbird Review presents fine writing by contributors ranging from new poets and essayists to fully established literary figures. We are committed to portraying the beauty, culture and challenges of the human experience through literature and art, and cross-cultural writing in all forms.

We offer you this labor of love in hopes you'll find a measure of solace, a touch of peace, and a dash of joy during the time you spend between these covers.

— Charles Redner • Publisher • Spring, 2017

LUIS ALBERTO URREA

Some Thoughts on *Into the Beautiful North*
by Luis Alberto Urrea

I had spent 25 years on *The Hummingbird's Daughter* and its sequel, *Queen of America.* Those who know me already know that many of those years were passages of duress. If you have ever wandered into the world of spirits and shamans, you know what I'm talking about. That's another book for the ghost section of the library. And I had somehow penetrated the world of the US Border Patrol and the human smugglers on the border for *The Devil's Highway.* While writing it, I was told three different times by law enforcement officers that I would be killed by the bad guys. I was also embroiled in a car crash with cocaine smugglers from Mexico. Stress and bad mojo all around, and no way to know if any of those books would be taken seriously. Apparently, they were.

In the interim, I had written a searing novel about barrio violence that my publisher rejected. Too dark. All this left me in some authorial tatters. It was time for fun. Time to laugh out loud.

So that was what I set out to do. My orders to myself were: coffee every day, loud music, and don't leave the desk until you laugh. I didn't know if I'd ever publish it. What I did know is that I would not abandon my focus on writing of Witness. Hey–if you're not trying to change the world, stay in bed. My wife says I have a Jesus complex. Maybe it's just a Bono complex.

The book arose from news articles about Mexican towns emptied of able-bodies men. Women in these towns were filling a vacuum in leadership left by the men who had, of course, all come north. Suddenly, there was a wave of feminism happening–a kind of folk feminism. Not a lot of critical theory, but lots of need. So we were seeing women as mayors, police chiefs, school directors, even projectionists in movie houses. In many of these smaller towns, it was for the first time.

There I was, with my giant coffee mug, Mexican rock playing, and these thoughts in my head. I immediately knew that my family's home town in Sinaloa would be the model for the town in this book. It had always been my personal Macondo (*One Hundred Years of Solitude*)–Rosario, on the mighty Baluarte River. For much of my life, it remained the hottest place I had ever lived for any amount of time. And the most hilarious. I was ahead on smiles from the first word typed. But I knew I'd need some literary leeway, so I fictionalized it by called it Tres Camarones. Yes, Three Shrimp. Why? Because it's stupid. And because the peculiar humor of the intellectuals in Rosario would find such a meaningless name funny. (Sinaloa has a town notoriously named Palo Cagado. That would be: Shit On A Stick in English. Recently cleaned up as Nombre Feo. Ugly Name. How could you not find humor in this milieu?)

Note: the movie theater that kicks off the adventure in the book is my uncle's movie theater, El Cine Pedro Infante. As soon as I had hit on the town and the theater, I populated the book with homages to real people. Aunt Irma, for example, is my real Aunt Irma. Mexico's Women's Bowling National Champion. If you'd like to get a gander at Rosario, I have a graphic novel called *Mr. Mendoza's Paintbrush*. It was drawn by Christopher Cardinale, and it shows Rosario in all its funky glory.

The book came out to modest success and generally good reviews, spiced up by a few bad ones and one rabid Monty-Pythonesque savaging that still make me laugh. Then faded into its modest mid-life. But a miracle happened. The NEA picked it for their Big Read program. Suddenly, all over the country, whole cities, towns and Universities were tackling it. It came roaring back to life. And after a couple of years of this, other countries started to show interest. Then TNT network came along and are as of this writing preparing a television series.

My little afternoon personal therapy found new life. And my original plan to laugh out loud was fulfilled. My deeper plan, against all odds, also is finding its effect: to make readers looking for a popular read (as opposed to "literary fiction") care for and even root for people they might otherwise look down on ... or be told by political figures are bad people. There is no them. There is only us.

L.A.U.
Chicagoland, 2017

FROM *INTO THE BEAUTIFUL NORTH*
By Luis Alberto Urrea

Sur
Chapter One

The bandidos came to the village at the worst possible time. Of course, everyone in Mexico would agree that there is no particularly good time for bad men to come to town. But Tres Camarones was unguarded on that late summer's day when so many things had already changed. And everything that remained was about to change forever.

Nobody in the village liked change. It had taken great civic upheaval to bring electricity to Tres Camarones, for example. Until 1936, ice came in big trucks, and fathers took their sons to observe it when it slid down the ramps in great clear blocks. It took the visionary mayor, Garcí a-García the First, to see the potential in electrical power, and he had lobbied for two years to have the wires strung from far Villaunión. Still, there were holdouts a good decade after Tres Camarones had begun to glow with yellow light. Such stalwarts relied on candles, kerosene lamps, and small bonfires in the street. These blazes, though festive, blocked the scant traffic and the trucks bearing beer and sides of beef, and Garcí a-García had to resort to the apocalyptic stratagem of banning street fires entirely. Denounced as an Antichrist, he was promptly defeated in the next election. Later, he was reelected: even if his policies had been too modernizing for some, the residents of Tres Camarones realized that a new mayor meant change, and change was the last thing they wanted. Progress might be inevitable, but there was no reason they should knuckle under without a fight.

True, the occasional hurricane devastated the low-lying forest and semitropical jungles and reformed the beaches. Often, parts of the town were washed away or carried out to sea. But the interior clock of evolution in Tres Camarones was set only to these cataclysms of nature. And then, the peso dropped in value. Suddenly there was no work. All the shrimp were shipped north, tortillas became too expensive to eat, and people started to go hungry. *We told you change was bad, the old-timers croaked.*

Nobody had heard of the term *immigration.* Migration, to them, was when the tuna and the whales cruised up the coast, or when Guacamaya parrots flew up from the south. Traditionalists voted to revoke electricity, but it was far too late for that. No woman in town would give up her refrigerator, her electric fan, or her electric iron. So the men started to go to el norte. Nobody knew what to say. Nobody knew what to do. The modern era had somehow passed Tres Camarones by, but this new storm had found a way to siphon its men away, out of their beds and into the next century, into a land far away.

***

The bandidos came with the sunrise, rolling down the same eastern road that had once brought the ice trucks. There were two of them. They had to drive south from Mazatlán, which was at least an hour and forty minutes away, then creak off the highway and take the cutoff toward the coast. Explosions of parrots, butterflies, and hummingbirds parted before them. They didn't notice.

One of them was an agent of the Policía Estatal, the dreaded Sinaloa State Police. He earned $150 a month as a cop. The drug cartel in the north of the state paid him $2,500 a month as an advisory fee. He got a $15,000 bonus each Christmas.

The other was a bottom-level narco who, nevertheless, was the state cop's boss. What he needed to really get ahead in his game was a territory to call his own, but the cartel had the state sewn up, and there was no room for him in Baja California, Sonora, or Chihuahua. He had hit the drug gangster's glass ceiling and it irked him, because he looked so damned good. The boys called him Scarface. He liked that. In spite of the awful heat and soggy air of the coastal swamplands, he wore a white sport jacket and regarded the world through mirrored sunglasses, sucking on a cinnamon toothpick.

Neither of the two bandidos enjoyed this bucolic trip to the bottomlands. But the one in the jacket had gotten a cell phone call from Culiacán that there were gringo surfos camping on the beach who were in need of some bud. He shook his head as he looked out at the stupid mango trees: all this trouble for marijuana. "It's a job," Scarface said. The cop snorted.

Scarface wore his irritating chrome .45 automatic in a shoulder rig. It made his armpit and ribs into a swamp of perspiration. It was against the law for a Mexican to carry an automatic weapon, though he didn't even think about it. His partner wore a uniform and had a heavy Bulldog .44 in a Sam Browne holster—the narco could smell its leather and was irritated by its squeaking as the car bumped along the bad road.

The holster squeak was the closest they could get to a theme song. There was nothing on the radio out here except the crappy Mexican music on AM.

"Me gusta Kanye West," the narco said, snapping off the radio.

The state cop said, "Diddy es mejor."

"¡Diddy!" cried Scarface.

They argued for a few moments.

Soon, they reverted to silence. The cop turned up the AC. His gun belt squealed.

"Dios mío," Scarface sighed. "I hate the country."

The men kept their windows rolled up, but they could still smell the ripe effluent of mud and clams and pigsties and spawning fish in green water. They wrinkled their noses. "What is that?" the cop asked. "Boiling mangos?" They shook their heads, greatly offended. The other one pointed.

"Outhouses!" he scoffed.

They couldn't believe it! These towns were so backward, Emiliano Zapata and a bunch of revolutionaries could ride through at any moment and fit right in. The bandidos, a generation removed from outhouses, sneered at the skinny dogs and the absurd starving roosters that panicked as the car rolled over oyster shells and brushed aside sugarcane and morning glory vines. The rubes down here had apparently never heard of blacktop. It was all dirt roads and cobblestones. No tourists.

They were slightly pleased, yet jealous, when they noted one of the small houses had a satellite dish.

As in most neighborhoods of most tropical Mexican villages, the walls of the homes in town went right to the edge of the street. Walls were wavery and one block long, and several doors could be found in each. Each door denoted another address. The windows had big iron railings and wooden shutters. Bougainvillea cascaded from several rooflines. Trumpet flowers. Lantana. The bandidos knew that the back of each house was a courtyard with a tree and an open kitchen and some chickens and an iguana or two. Laundry. On the street side, the walls were great splashes of color. One address might be white, and the next might be pale blue and the next vivid red with a purple door. Sometimes, two primary colors were divided by a bright green drainpipe or a vibrating line where the colors clashed and the human eye began to rattle in its socket.

The big police LTD rolled down the streets like a jaguar sniffing for its prey. The two visitors came out of the narrow alleys into the open space of the town plazuela, a tawdry gazebo and a bunch of trees with their trunks whitewashed. On the other side of the square, they spied a restaurant: TAQUERIA E INTERNET "LA MANO CAIDA."

"The Fallen Hand Taco Shop? What kind of name is that?" the cop asked.

"It's an Internet café, too," the narco reminded him.

"Jesus Christ."

"Let's get out of here quick," his partner said. "I want to catch the beisbol game in Mazatlán tonight." He spit out his toothpick.

They creaked to a halt and could hear the music blasting out of the Fallen Hand before they even opened the car's doors.

Chapter Two

Here came Nayeli, late for work again, dancing through town on her way to the Fallen Hand. She didn't mean to dance—it was just that everywhere she went, she swung and swayed, and it was all she could do to keep herself from running. She had been the star forward of the Tres Camarones girls' soccer team for four years, and even though she'd been out of high school for a year, she was still in shape. Her dark legs were hard with muscle and she still wore her tiny school uniform skirt, so everybody could admire them. Besides, clothes didn't grow on trees. Nayeli was dreaming of leaving town again. She wanted to see anything, everything. Wanted to go where lights changed color, where airplanes lumbered overhead and the walls of great buildings were covered in television screens like in that Bill Murray Japanese movie they'd seen at the Cine Pedro Infante the week before. She wanted shimmering lines of traffic in city rain. She was eager to see a concert, ride a train, wear fancy clothes, and sip exotic coffees on a snowy boulevard. She had seen elevators in a thousand movies, and she longed to ride one, though not on the roof of one like Jackie Chan.

Sometimes, she dreamed of going to the United States—"Los Yunaites," as the people of the town called them—to find her father, who had left and never come back. He traded his family for a job, and then he stopped writing or sending money. She didn't like to think about him. People kidded her that she never stopped smiling, and it made her look flirty, but thinking about him made the smile fade. She walked faster.

Nayeli was coming from Aunt Irma's campaign headquarters, located in the stifling kitchen of Irma's house on Avenida Francisco Madero. Irma, sick and tired of the ancient mayor of Tres Camarones ("That smelly old man!" she often complained), was making history by running to replace him in the next election. It would be a first: Irma García Cervantes, the first female Municipal President of Tres Camarones. It had an excellent ring to it. She had leadership experience—Aunt Irma was Sinaloa's retired Lady Bowling Champion—and she was used to celebrity and the heat of the public's attentions. If political power was not her destiny, she reasoned, it could only mean the Good Virgin herself had dictated that Mexico should continue its slide into chaos and ruin.

One of Nayeli's main tasks was to write with fat sidewalk chalk, "¡Aunt Irma for President!" on walls all around Tres Camarones. As campaign manager, she earned twenty pesos a week, proving that Aunt Irma, too, had that affliction detested by Sinaloans yet epidemic in proportion. They called it "el codo duro": the hard elbow, or the unbending elbow—unbending when it came time to spend money.

Twenty pesos! You couldn't even afford corn tortillas anymore on twenty pesos. The Americans were buying up all the maize for fuel, and none of the rancheros could afford to use it for food. What did come down to the people was too expensive to purchase. So Nayeli danced on down the street to her second job, serving tacos and soft drinks at La Mano Caída.

Let's eat," the cop said. They had gotten restless, waiting for the damned Americano surfos to show up. They had a brick of pot in the trunk of their car, and the clock was ticking. He tapped on the bar.

Tacho, the Fallen Hand's taco master, glowered.

"What you got?" the cop asked.

Tacho was tired of the thugs. They glared too much for his taste.

"Food," he said.

The narco smiled.

"You're kind of mouthy for a queer."

Tacho shrugged.

"He's a queer?" the cop said.

"He's wearing eye makeup," said Scarface.

"I thought he was one of those emo kids you hear about." The cop shrugged.

Emo sucks," Scarface muttered.

"I like Diddy," the cop reminded him.

Tacho had just about had it, but suddenly, Nayeli burst through the doors.

"You're late!" Tacho scolded.

"I'm sorry, Tachito mi amor," she called, automatically falling into her flirting banter with him. "Tachito machito mi angelito."

The gunmen snorted: Little Tacho, my little macho, my little angel. That was too rich. They nudged each other.

"You're macho, eh?" the cop said. "A macho angel."

They giggled. "¿Eres joto?" the narco asked Tacho, because if this hot little girl was talking to him like that, he might not be a queer after all.

Tacho made eyes at Nayeli. She hurried to tie on a white apron. She saw the silver glint of the narco's .45 peeking out from behind his jacket.

"Take a table," Tacho said. "No need for gentlemen like yourselves to sit at the bar."

He smiled at them—it looked as if he were getting a tooth pulled, but anything to get them across the room from him. He didn't want to have them near enough to smell their tacky cologne. One of them was wearing Old Spice!

They sat at one of Tacho's quaking little tin Carta Blanca tables.

"What do you recommend?" the cop asked Nayeli.

"Tacho's fried-oyster tortas are legendary," she replied.

"Sounds good."

She turned away.

12

He grabbed her hand and pulled her back. "You," he said. "You're under arrest."

She felt a pure cold bolt of panic.

"Excuse me?"

"You're under suspicion"—he sneered—"of stealing my heart."

He let her go and sent her back across the room on a gale of laughter. Her face was burning. Tacho whispered to her, "Viejo feo." Ugly old man. It was one of his favorite insults.   "Good one," the narco was saying.

They kept laughing, wiping their eyes.

"Hey!" he called. "Girl! Bring us some drinks!"

Tacho sighed. "It's going to be one of those days," he said.

Nayeli fished two beers out of the vat of ice at the end of the bar.

The men scared her. She tried to think about other things when she was tense or afraid, better days, before things had turned so sad, before everyone had become so poor.

She opened the beer bottles, served them, and rushed back to the end of the bar while Tacho started frying up the oysters.

The narco pulled his big pistol out of the shoulder holster and laid it on the table. He held open his jacket and flapped his arm a little. He turned his head and eyed Nayeli. He patted the gun and smiled at her.

"Está caliente, la chaparra," he noted.

The cop glanced over at her to see how hot the shortie really was. They studied her legendary legs. Her bright white teeth against the deep cinnamon brown of her skin made her smile radiate like moonlight on water.

"A little dark," he said. "But she'll do."

He winked at her and sipped his icy beer.

***

Nobody was quite sure if Tres Camarones was in Sinaloa or Nayarit, since the state line wavered in and out of the mangrove swamps and lagoons thereabouts. There was no major highway going through; there was no local police station, no hotel or tourist trap. No harbor, no television or radio station, no police station, no supermarket. The high school was in Villaunión, a long sweaty bus trip away. The church was small and full of fruit bats. Of course, there was a small Carta Blanca beer distributor, but come to think of it, the office had shut down when the men went north to find work. It was easier to float a boat down the tributaries of the Baluarte River than it was to drive the dirt road spur that angled southwest off the highway to Rosario. At any rate, nobody had ever worried about maps—on the official Pemex highway guides, Tres Camarones didn't even exist.

The American boys who started it all by making a peeved chibacall to their Mazatlán connection, seeking a key of gold bud, were on spring break from some college in California. They had wandered down the coast, looking for good surfing and party spots, and they'd made the error of picking the sugar-white beaches outside Tres Camarones for their camp. The locals could have told them— but didn't—that the picturesque beaches belied a brutal drop-off, and the waves hammered against a nearly vertical wall of underwater mud. Other hazards abounded. The nearest popular beach was called Caimanero because big alligators lurked in the foul freshwater swamps behind the shore—not a spot for frolic. Portuguese man-of-wars floated onto the beaches all summer, killing everything they could sting. There was a spoiling porpoise carcass on the sand to bear testimony to their powers. The safest salt water in that whole region was in the shallow turquoise lagoons where the women went crabbing with floating straw baskets full of scrabbling *jaibas*, the big crabs taking their last little sea cruise before landing in the cooking pot. But you couldn't surf a tranquil lagoon.

It wasn't like the people hadn't seen Americanos. Tres Camarones had been beset by tides of missionaries from Southern California. But the Jesús Es Mi Fiel Amigo Sunday School and the End Times Templo Evangélico had finally closed down for lack of converts. The "youth center" went back to being a muffler shop that was also closed because its owner had gone to Florida to pick oranges. For a short while, an ashram run by a Wisconsin woman named Chrystal, who was in constant channeling-contact with the Venusian UFO-naut P'taak, rose north of town. Several local workers had made good wages working on Chrystal's pink cement pyramid on her leased forty acres of scrub and pecan trees. But the local water cut short P'taak's mission to the world, and Chrystal rushed back to Sheboygan with typhoid and amebic dysentery. After Chrystal's personal rapture, the Jehovah's Witnesses, known as Los

Testigos de Jeová, were forced to leave town when the heroic local bowling champion, Aunt Irma, unleashed her devilish tongue upon them and christened them Los Testículos de Jeová. The Witnesses, deeply offended, packed up their Spanish editions of *The Watchtower* and abandoned the heathens to their grisly fate.

***

Scarface tossed aside his napkin. The lime juice and Cholula sauce were better when you sucked them off your fingers. The table was a wasteland of empty plates. He stood.

"Where are these pinches gringos!" he shouted.

The state cop checked his watch, put down his beer bottle, and turned to glare at Tacho as if the proprietor were the surfers' secretary.

"We are busy men," he warned.

"I've been here an hour!" Scarface complained.

Tacho shrugged.

"You know how Americans are," he said. "Always late. On their own time."

Scarface kicked back his chair and grabbed his gun. He held it down by his side, as if deciding whether Tacho and Nayeli needed shooting. "If the surfos show up, tell them next time we see them, they each get a bullet in the head. Understand? I don't like to be kept waiting."

"Sí, señor," Nayeli replied.

The bad men strode out and got back into their car. Scarface pulled a fresh cinnamon toothpick out of his breast pocket. He took off the cellophane wrapper, dropped it on the floor, and popped the toothpick in his mouth. It waggled up and down. "Nice town," he said. "No cops."

He adjusted his lapels.

"No men, did you notice?"

He smiled.

"A vato like me could make a real killing here."

He wiped his sunglasses on his shirt and put them back on.

"Watch yourselves," he called out the window.

They drove away without paying.

Chapter Three

As the bandidos prowled the town and its outskirts, Tacho and Nayeli went about their day. Mopping the cement floor, sweeping the sidewalk in front, slicing limes, and peeling mangos. But mostly, they did what Mexicans in every small town in Mexico did: they circled their own history.

Nayeli was thinking about the missionaries. Well, she was thinking about one of them. The one saint—Missionary Matt. All of Nayeli's notorious girlfriends loved Missionary Matt. He was the first blond boy any of them had ever seen in person. They could claim that the vapid white-boy handsomeness of El Brad Pitt or El Estip McQueen at the cinema didn't move them, but up close, it was a different story. A real live blue-eyed white boy was their own romantic freak show. Matt's nose peeled. They had never seen a peeling nose. It was precious.

Matt sneaked away from his pastoral duties every night and crept into the Cine Pedro Infante. Nayeli's girlfriends were not the only ones who sat in restless groups all around him, tittering over his slightest jest. Even mothers and aunties tittered, "¡Ay, Mateo!" whenever he said anything.

That boy was movie crazy.

Matt had endeared himself to the many girls in town by writing their names phonetically on four-by-six-inch cards. When he left, he left behind a hundred broken hearts as he distributed these well-thumbed cards to his sweethearts as farewell gifts, with his address and phone number written on the back of each.

The card was the closest thing to a love letter Nayeli had ever received. She pulled it out for inspection, the ink a little diffuse from her sweat. It read:

nah /YELL/ ee

Beneath this, it said:
Love, Matt!

Then an address and a phone number that started with an 858 prefix.

Love, Nayeli thought. She knew enough English to know that. *Love. Was it love-love? Like, LOVE? Or was it just love, like*

16

mi-amigo-Mateo-love, like I love my sister or my puppy or peanut butter cups love?

"Hello?" Tacho said. "Work? Like, sometime today?"

"Oh, you," she said dreamily.

Tacho raised his hands and seemed to beseech the universe.

Nayeli kept Missionary Matt's card tucked in her kneesock along with the sole, tattered postcard her father had sent her from a place called KANKAKEE, ILLINOIS. It showed a wild turkey gazing with deep paranoia out of a row of cornstalks. Before he'd fled to KANKAKEE, Don Pepe had been the only police officer in Tres Camarones. Mostly, he directed traffic and inspected the rare car wreck on the eastern road. Nayeli's father had been gone three years. When it really got hot, and she was sweaty enough to threaten the ink altogether, she reluctantly tucked the two cards into her mirror at home.

She wandered out on the sidewalk and swept listlessly. The scant heavy river breeze stirred her tiny skirt. Boys used to whistle at Nayeli when she went by, but she'd been noticing a silence in the streets. Perhaps nineteen was already too old. Everything was changing for her. There was nowhere for a champion futbolista to go if she was a girl. And it was out of the question for her to head off to Culiacán or somewhere else expensive to attend the university. Her mother took in laundry—but, really, all the old women of Tres Camarones took in laundry. It would take many more dirty and lazy people to sustain the home laundry industry. Fortunately, Nayeli and her mother received some assistance from the formidable Tía Irma— the future Municipal President. Tía Irma's pro bowling winnings had been sufficiently vast that she had actually invested most of her money, and she was further comfortably attended to by monthly retirement checks from her hard years at the canneries. The checks were modest, but she didn't need much more than Domino cigarettes, the occasional bottle of rum, and a steady diet of Tacho's tacos and tortas.

It was Tía Irma, known to the notorious girlfriends as La Osa—the She-Bear—who had pushed Nayeli into fútbol. And it was both Irma and Don Pepe who had enrolled Nayeli in Dr. Matsuo Grey's martial arts dojo when the other girls were taking dance lessons for the various pageants and balls at the Club de Leones. Karate, Tía Irma insisted, was good for the legs. Power on the field.

17

But Nayeli was not fooled. To La Osa, life and love were war, and she expected Nayeli to win as many battles as possible.

Aunt Irma wanted her to beat up men.

Missionary Matt had taught Nayeli a term for Tía Irma: *Es muy hard-core, La Osa.*

***

¡Ay, Mateo!" Nayeli said out loud. He was on some glorious California beach, and she was at Tacho's.

It was a job, at least. It gave her money for shoes or movie tickets at the cine. Since Matt had donated his Satellite laptop to Tacho when he left, the taquería had been transformed into an Internet café.

Nayeli sashayed in and tossed the broom into the corner.

"I'm going on el Internet," she announced.

"Do you think I pay you to play on the computer all day?" Tacho scolded.

"Yes."

"¡Cabrona!"

Tacho was cranky like this with all the girls. It was part of his routine. A man like Tacho had to learn to survive in Mexico, and he had learned to re-create himself in bright colors, in large attitudes, thus becoming a cherished character. If you wanted to achieve immortality, or at least acceptance, in Tres Camarones, the best thing to do was become an amazing fixture. It was very macho to be a ne'er-do-well, even if you were gay. That's why mewling missionaries didn't stand a chance. Being meek wasn't macho. There was no legend there.

For years, the joke about Tacho's "kind"—los jotos—was that they suffered from the affliction of "la mano caída." The fallen hand, the cartoony limp wrist of the gay man in the common pantomime: just the phrase made people laugh. Except for Tacho. He didn't accept being called "faggot" by anybody (except his girls), and he certainly didn't feel that he was limp-wristed in any way. So he threw it back in their faces by naming his establishment the Fallen Hand. Genius! Even the most macho men in town had embraced him immediately, because he was wittier than they were, and because of this, somehow more macho.

That was years ago. Lately, the Mano Caída mostly attracted bored old ladies with very little money, or Nayeli's troublesome bratty girls—and they never spent a peso. All they wanted to do was look at gringo boys on the Internet. He sighed. What a life.

At least he also sold women's shoes from his back bedroom over on Avenida Benito Juárez. Nayeli wasn't the only one who could work Mateo's computer! Indeed, Tacho had found eBay, and he had begun his second career with the help of Tía Irma's American Express card. Thanks to Tacho, Tres Camarones was now treated to a monthly visit from bright yellow DHL delivery trucks, an exotic touch that made the citizens feel cosmopolitan.

Tacho and Nayeli shared a lust for big cities—any big cities. They used the computer to spy on New York, London, Madrid, Paris. Sometimes, after work, they climbed on the roof of the restaurant to watch the bats. They made believe that clouds were the Manhattan skyline.

***

Oh no," groaned Tacho, "here come the rest of them."

The notorious girlfriends—what was left of them—were walking up the sidewalk. They were yelling, "¡Adios!" to everybody they knew on the street. People in Tres Camarones didn't say hello, they said good-bye.

Nayeli looked out and grinned. There were only three of them left, but they liked to brag that they were the best of the bunch. Cuquis Cristerna had moved to Culiacán. Sachiko Uzeta Amano had gone to Mexico City to learn how to make movies. María de los Angeles Hernandez Osuna was studying to be a doctor in Guadalajara. Now it was just Nayeli, Yoloxochitl, and Verónica.

Yoloxochitl's phonetic Missionary Matt card read:
YO-LOW / SO-*sheet*

He called her "Yo-Yo," which amused him no end. Her parents had been infected with folklore mania, a real danger among liberal Mexicans with college educations. Her father had made it through one year of university, and thus well-connected to his Toltec past, he and Yoloxochitl's mother had decided to christen their off-spring with Nahuatl names. Fortunately for everyone, they'd had only two children. Unfortunately for her older brother, they had named him Tlaloc. Young Tlaloc didn't enjoy being known as the

Rain God—every time he went to pee, his friends made relentless jokes—so he changed the name to Lalo before he went north with his father to become nameless.

Matt had already known how to say Verónica, but just to make her feel good, he'd made a card out for her, too.

ver-OH! / knee-kah

Lately Yoloxochitl had been working as a pin tender at the three-lane bowling alley down by the statue of Benito Juárez. Verónica worked as a shrimp peeler in the stinking estuaries north of town. Neither one liked her job. Too much sweat. Yoloxochitl wore her faded El Tri rocanrol T-shirt and some gaucho pants Tacho had sold her for half price. Her mother had saved for a year to get her out of glasses; her contact lenses had unleashed the fashion model inside her. She was carrying another one of her paperback books. Yolo—as the girls all called her—was always reading.

As usual, everybody was staring at Verónica, the only goth girl in Sinaloa. She had made her face pale with various ointments and creams, and she had painted her eyelids dark, her lips black, her nails black. She wore a long black skirt that must have been stifling, yet she managed to radiate cool air when she walked by. Verónica ironed her hair so it hung down like a sheet of satin. Her hair was already utterly black, but she also dyed it with Black No. 1 rinse just like her heroes in Type O Negative, whose videos she'd seen with Nayeli on YouTube.

It was much harder for girls to become astounding characters in the fabric of Tres Camarones culture—they were mostly, if they were eccentric, seen as outrageous monsters—but Verónica's every public appearance was a shock.

She had been a goth for three months; before that, she had dreamed of being a pop star in revealing hot pants and see-through blouses of televised Latin American variety shows. She was going to dye her hair that plasticine coppery color that passed for blond among Mexican starlets. Only the notorious girlfriends noted that she'd gone goth after her father and mother had died.

Everyone called her La Vampira.

The girls burst through the door, popping gum and clanking bracelets.

"Tachito, mi flor!" trilled Yolo.

Normally, Tacho would flick anyone who called him a flower with his deadly washcloth.   "Tramp," he replied, not meanly.

"Yolo!" Nayeli called.

"¿Qué onda, morra?" Yolo replied, delighting in street slang. Sounding like a city tough was so rocanrol. She was the best student among them—if she had been able to, she would have studied dentistry in college. She, too, was a soccer star, though Nayeli had overshadowed her on the field.

"Hola, Nayeli," sighed La Vampira.

"Vampi!" Nayeli said. "How is life, Vampi?"

"Sad," said La Vampira. She pulled a rosary from her black beaded clutch purse (Tacho's fashion emporium, 155 pesos). The beads rattled on the table. "I don't know how much more I can take."

Yolo and Nayeli looked at each other and rolled their eyes. Tacho, a sucker for the goth routine, made up a small bowl of mango and pineapple and orange slices with red chile powder on them, and sat with La Vampira and poked toothpicks into the fruit.

"Eat," he said. "You've got to eat, my angel."

"Oh… Tacho…" she breathed. She squeezed his hand weakly.

"She's an angel?" muttered Nayeli. "Angel of death, maybe."

Yolo snorted.

"You snorted," Nayeli said.

"I so did not snort."

Nayeli clicked the keys and opened a video of a skateboarder getting hit in the crotch by his board on Google Video. She made a face and switched Web sites. Ah! Captain Jack Sparrow. Yolo leaned against Nayeli's shoulder. She turned to La Vampi and said, "Oye, Vampi. La Nayeli is going to marry Johnny Depp."

"Mmm, Capitán Yack Esparrow," Vampi said.

"Oh, yes," Tacho agreed. "Es muy caliente, el Capitán Yack." Verónica made a face.   "Me encanta," Nayeli said. "I love him."

"Me, too," Tacho said.

"Yack Esparrow," Vampi said, "needs a bath."

She waved her hand dismissively.

"Besides," she added, "I can only marry one man."

"Not again," muttered Nayeli.

She grumbled and went to YouTube. Verónica had never even seen "gothic" people before she had watched Nayeli work Tacho's computer, but as soon as she saw wan boys in mascara, she was lost. Type O Negative was awesome, or "chido," as she put it. The Sisters of Mercy put her way around the bend. And now this. Nayeli huffed, then typed in "The 69 Eyes." Thinking: *Why do I do this?*

"What does that mean?" Tacho asked.

"He must have sixty-nine eyes," Yolo said.

"Who does?"

"Him," said Nayeli, pointing to the goth band on the screen, and at the cadaver sitting in their midst.

"He always wears sunglasses," Vampi marveled. "His name is Jyrki."

"The glasses hide all those eyeballs," Yolo said.

"¿Qué?" asked Tacho.

"Here we go," Nayeli said, mouse clicking to call up Vampi's favorite song, "Gothic Girl."

The girls started to dance. Tacho thought this Jyrki person sounded like he was dead, but he sounded comfortable being a corpse, even happy.

"Dance with me, boy," Nayeli commanded.

Tacho took Nayeli's hand and tried a cumbia to the music. La Vampi went crazy and started jumping up and down, bobbing her head from side to side. In her heavily accented English, she sang, "I love my gothic girl!" Well, what she said was: "Ay lob myng goddig gorrl." And everyone laughed.

***

Nayeli didn't get home until ten o'clock. When she came in the door, her mother said, "What were you doing?"

Nayeli said, "Nothing. Just another day at work, Mami."

"How is Tacho?"

"Fine."

Nayeli ate some calabazas and a glass of milk, then went to bed in front of her ancient electric fan. The geckos chirped on the wall above her bed.

Her mother called, "We're going to the lagoon tomorrow."

"Awesome!" Nayeli called. What she shouted was: "Chido."
But her mother did not know what that newfangled word meant.

"Night, Mami."

"Good night, m'ijita."

Nayeli rolled her head on the hot pillow. She was asleep
before she knew it was happening. She dreamed that she lived in a
big white house, surrounded by trees and fountains. There was snow
on the distant mountain range. Her horses were white, and the swans
in her lake floated serenely as the maids served tea. She had English
muffins with strawberry jam on a silver tray. She spoke perfect
English. She wore a long gown and ate ice cream when she was done
with the muffins. Her husband, Johnny Depp, had gold teeth, black
eyeliner, and waist-length hair. "Tomorrow," he said with a metallic
grin, "we will go to Kankakee."

Chapter Four

Tía Irma headed down the sidewalk like a parade float, and
they hurried to keep up with her.

"Crab day!" she called as she motored along on squeaky
shoes, thinking the people who smiled at Nayeli were smiling at her.
Crabbing was like going to heaven. A whole day immersed in the
clear lagoon, with barrels of ice full of soda and beer, the thatch-
roofed huts in the sand swinging with hammocks, the big pots
boiling crabs to be eaten on stiff fried tortillas. There was nothing
better than crab day.

They boarded the two boats at the sloping little dock. Nayeli
had stopped at the graves of her grandparents and pulled a few
weeds, shy red-legged tarantulas feeling their way between the
monuments.

The river water was deep green and sluggish as it moved by,
carrying pollen and leaves. The banks here were dark mud flecked
with a scatter of white shells. Fat green frogs, the eternally grinning
type destined to be shellacked into bizarre poses while wearing
mariachi hats and holding toy trumpets and guitars and then sold in
tourist traps all over Mexico, jostled lazily in the dappled shadows.
Brilliant egrets and blue herons stalked the reeds on the shore.

La Osa settled into the first boat, tipping it alarmingly but
refusing to note the hubbub she caused. She wore a vast straw hat

upon her head, and she snapped her 10,000th picture of a tree orchid with her ancient plastic Kodak. "Each flower," she lectured, "as distinct as a snowflake!" Not that any of them had ever seen a snowflake.

Behind Tía Irma sat Nayeli's mother—a well-known hypochondriac since her husband left.

"María," Irma said. "How are you today?"

"Oh," Nayeli's mother said. "Not very well."

Irma snapped, "You've been dying for years. Why don't you get it over with?"

In an hour, they had come to the bend in the river where the boats could be beached and tied to bushes, and the party disembarked and grunted over the slope, breaking suddenly, amazingly, from jungly dark to a dazzling white cove that had at its center a wide oblong lagoon of brightest turquoise. Beyond the far end of the lagoon, the thundering surf of the deadly beach could be seen, dark ocean water exploding in spray and foam with a relentless basso roar. Everything seemed woven of purest sunlight. The coconut palms bobbed with their bright green harvests nestled among the silky-looking fronds. Beyond the coconuts, hibiscus trees stood twenty feet tall, burning with crimson blossoms. Little thatched huts sagged at jaunty angles, and Nayeli wasted no time getting to them, prying open their storage boxes, and unfurling the mesh hammocks stored inside. The breeze never stilled: miraculously, no one could tell how hot it was, or how humid. The faint whiffs of rotting porpoise occasionally spoiled the Edenic effect, but otherwise they had reached the most perfect spot in the world.

Irma said to María, her niece: "Your husband should have come here before he left. He would have stayed home. ¡En México lindo!"

Nayeli's mother replied, "You cannot eat beauty."

***

Yolo and Nayeli were in the lagoon. The water only came up to their hips. Tiny fish sniffed and nibbled at their thighs. Nayeli's hair was pulled back in a loose ponytail. Yolo had cut hers for the summer. On the white sand, Tacho had a fire going, and he was boiling seawater with onions and secret sauces. Yolo nudged Nayeli:

24

Tacho was wearing a cloth wrapped around his waist like a sarong. The girls laughed.

They moved deeper into the lagoon. They watched their bellies and hips wobble and distend in the water. The reflected light made Nayeli's skin look white. She regarded it fondly.   Yolo said, "Remember when Mateo the Missionary came here with us?"

"Ay, Matt," Nayeli sighed.

"He was so cute," Yolo said.

"That crab pinched his toe."

"He was screaming."

"I had to bite the crab's claw open."

"Nayeli," Yolo said, "you were always the strong one."

"Do you think he remembers us?"

Yolo gestured at her own body.

"Who could forget this?" she boasted.

But Yolo wasn't blind—she'd seen Matt's eyes as he tried not to look Nayeli over.

"You kissed him," Yolo said, poking Nayeli in the arm.

"I did not!"

"Yes you did."

"No I didn't."

"No seas simple, Nayeli," Yolo scolded. "Everybody knows you kissed Mateo!"

Nayeli smiled.

"So?" she said.

Yolo gasped and splashed her.

"So it's true! You did kiss him!"

Nayeli shrugged with one shoulder.

"Maybe."

The kiss—Matt would remember that, she was certain. His mouth was delicious, with his cherry cola lip balm. Soft lips. Those soft curls, too, smelling like apple juice from that girls' shampoo he used. She liked to think of Matt's mouth as having American lips— labios Americanos. It could be a power ballad by Maná.

**

La Osa's comadres were across the water, moving toward them. Everyone was hunting for crabs. They each carried a stick. Between each pair of women floated a big straw basket. The notorious girlfriends' open basket already held ten furiously scrabbling crabs. The armored creatures wrestled one another, and when one seemed about to climb out of the basket and make its escape, the others would grab it and haul it back down into the endless battle.

"Look at that," Yolo said. "They never make it out."

"That's us," Nayeli said. "That's Mexico."

"Don't let your aunt hear you say that," Yolo warned.

They shuffled their feet along the bottom, stirring bright white clouds of sand that curled like smoke around their legs. Suddenly, a huge crab burst out of the sand and scuttled along the bottom. The girls yelped and ducked under water. Nayeli got to the crab first, and she pressed her stick to its back, holding it down. She carefully pinched it from behind—keeping well away from its powerful claws—and pulled it out of the water.

She shook her head to get the water out of her eyes and said, "Look at that!"

"Hey!" Yolo said. "¡Es hembra!"

A female.

Sure enough, the she-crab had a thick girdle of eggs plastered to her shell. Tacho would be delighted. Crab roe made a paste that moved him to orgasmic delight when he smeared it on a tortilla and soaked it in lemon juice and green salsa. Nayeli tossed her in the basket.

"Don't you feel guilty?" Yolo said. "Taking an expectant mother?"

"What, feel solidarity with a crab?" said Nayeli. Yolo was always simmering with revolutionary theories.

"In a way, she's our sister," Yolo insisted.

This was the trouble with straight-A students: they thought up positions and then thought up a thousand insane defenses for their instant policies.

"This crab is not my sister, Yolo. She is my lunch."

"She's no sister of mine—I'm not pregnant. This crab might be the sister of —" she started to say. Nayeli tried to think of a pregnant woman in Tres Camarones. "No sé quién. Who's pregnant?" Yolo snorted. She loved her ridiculous debates with Nayeli. They could talk in loops for hours on the merits of rock en español versus regaetón, or on the merits of fútbol versus beisbol.

26

They left poor Vampi suicidal with boredom when they got on their little jags.   "Crab!" Nayeli shouted, pointing.

This time Yolo beat her. She plunged under and worked her stick. It was a small male, but a small crab was still a tasty crab.

"That's a dozen," Nayeli said. "Let's take them to Tacho."

"Let's eat!" In her atrocious English, Nayeli said, *"Oh yeah, baby!"*

As they waded to shore, she said, "But who's pregnant? Seriously. I can't think of anybody."

Yolo thought.

They came out of the water, each of them holding a handle of the basket.

Yolo shrugged.
"I can't think of anybody, either," she said.

***

They squatted and gobbled their crabs, the women and Tacho. The shrimpers and boys sat at the far end of the lagoon, eating beans wrapped in tortillas and minding their own business. Occasionally, Tacho whistled, and one of the boys came running to open beer bottles and bring more crabs from the aromatic pot. La Osa made Tacho surrender three fat crabs to the boys so they could eat some, too. La Osa reminded herself of Benito Juárez at moments like that. She basked in affection for herself.

Nayeli waited for an opportune moment to ask the ladies, "Who's pregnant?"

"Not me," said Tacho.

They threw napkins and crab claws at him.

"Do you mean among us here?" La Osa said, patting her gut. "Because it's a little late for my comadres and me!" The older women chuckled. "You'd better not be trying to tell us anything," she warned. "You'd better not." She shook a crab leg at Nayeli.

La Osa finished another beer. Tacho hustled to fetch a fresh one and fished out a 7 Up for himself.

"Siete Oop," he announced.

"Why do you ask?" Aunt Irma finally said.

"When was Tres Camarones ever without babies?" Nayeli asked. "What an odd thing."

"Excuse me, girlfriends," Tacho interrupted. "You need men to make babies."

The old women nodded.

"What?" Nayeli said.

"Men," said Tacho.

"What are you talking about, machito?"

"Men. Didn't you notice?"

"Notice what?" "All the men are gone."
"Ridiculous."

"Oh, really."

"Jesus," Irma announced. "Is there anyone sillier than a teenage girl?"

The women and Tacho laughed out loud.

The girlfriends sat there glowering: they couldn't stand being called silly.

"All teenage girls ever notice," Irma said, "is their own little dramas. They're idiots." She used the graphic word babosadas, which denoted drool running down their chins but also suggested they were as stupid as babosos—slugs.

The girls were outraged.

"Are not!" they cried.

The women shook their heads.

"All gone," Irma said, making a puff with her lips. "Blown away. Off to the beautiful north." She took a swig of beer. "Welcome to the real world, children."

Nayeli stared at Yolo with her mouth hanging open.

All she could think was: *I'll show you who's stupid!*

Irma stood. She smacked the sand off her legs.

"I have one word for the men," she said as she stomped away. "Traitors!"

***

Nobody wanted to go home after their day at the beach, so they gathered at Tía Irma's house on the corner of 22 de Diciembre and Madero streets to watch her color television. La Osa set the TV in the window, facing the street, and the guests all hauled chairs out onto the cobbles so they could feel the breeze. They watched a telenovela featuring savage love among hacienda owners in Brazil. Then they watched a telenovela that featured savage love among cattle ranchers in Durango. It grew dark. Cicadas knocked themselves senseless against the television screen. Bats twirled above them like leaves flying in a windstorm. Passersby called, "¡Adios!" and all the watchers politely called back, "¡Adios!"

When a car came down the street, they all rose and moved their chairs up onto the curb so the car could pass. They didn't notice that one of the cars was the big narco LTD. "¡Adios!" they called, then moved their chairs back into the narrow street. Nayeli watched everybody on the curb. She looked very carefully. And she realized Tacho was right. There was nobody left in town but women, old men, and little children.

Adios.

CHARLES REDNER

A SORCERER TO MANY APPRENTICES:
AN AFTERNOON WITH ROBERT PINSKY

As we exit our car, a cool, February breeze – the official greeter at Point Loma Nazarene University – welcomes us. A lowering sun still warms this far edge of San Diego. Class is scheduled for 3:00 p.m. The "us" consists of three *Hummingbird Review* writers: Ellyn Maybe, Peggy Edwards, and I, lovers of all things poetic — which definitely includes Robert Pinsky, the Poet Laureate of the United States from 1997-2001 and the reason for our presence. A rare opportunity to observe Pinsky conduct a class has been provided by Dr. Dean Nelson, founder and director of the journalism program and facilitator of the university's 22nd Symposium by the Sea.

Students quietly file in and claim empty seats in a room prepared to accommodate forty. A chair brigade quickly floats forty additional seats, all filled before Pinsky utters a sound. Others will still have to stand along the rear wall and pray the fire marshal is busy elsewhere.

Dean Nelson beams with pride at the turnout while introducing his distinguished guest. Dressed in jeans and dark T-shirt, Pinsky stands ready to begin. The private class has been convened for the primary purpose of hearing three students' poems and Pinsky's critique.

Expecting an opening lecture, Pinsky surprises by saying, "I'll take questions from the students." The first question is about his wife: "What's it like living with a psychologist?"

Pinsky moves around the room, more like a dance instructor than a poet, his arms jutting out in every direction as he speaks. Talking about his wife's career path, in which she didn't decide on psychology until entering her forties, leads to his suggesting that whatever your major might be today, may not be the only career path you'll ultimately take.

He's asked where he gets his inspiration. He relays to an answer the late saxophonist Dexter Gordon gave to the same question: "Billie Holliday." Pinsky remembered Gordon went on to say that the music that thrilled him growing up was what he strove to provide an audience. He wanted you to *feel* what he felt listening to Holliday.

Pinsky next offers what he considers the best advice he can give any student of poetry: "Keep a journal – an anthology." He further explains, "One shouldn't just read a poem you love but sit at the computer and type it out. Keep a collection of what you like, what moves you, and you'll find that years later it may help you express what you want to say and possible how to say it. Learn from the masters and not exclusively from your own discipline – look to art, dance, music."

Pinsky relayed how much he enjoyed music as a teen and how he wants to give you that special feeling in everything he scribes.

He's asked about writer's block. "I don't like the word 'write,'" he says. He motions mouth-to-ear, mouth-to-ear, repeatedly saying we learn to speak as a child by listening and mouthing words, which he demonstrates with babbling baby talk. The audience erupts in laughter at his animated gyrations and gobble-gook sounds of a baby learning to speak. As an educator, he has learned how to capture a class with wit as well as wisdom. He is suggesting that one should think and speak, and the writing will follow. "I can do it in the shower," he adds. He refers back to Jonathan, remembering all the student names, as he responds. "Jonathan, you have considerable language skills, hear it, write it, you'll be fine."

He asks for another question. No student takes him up on it, so I ask, "Who's in your anthology?" Pinsky responds, "Throw out a letter." I offer, "R" knowing that he, like me, is a Rutgers grad. Grabbing his latest work, "Singing School", he searches for a poem. He settles on Edwin Arlington Robinson's "Eros Turannos":

Eros Turannos
By Edwin Arlington Robinson

She fears him, and will always ask
What fated her to choose him;
She meets in his engaging mask
All reasons to refuse him;
But what she meets and what she fears
Are less than are the downward years,
Drawn slowly to the foamless weirs
    Of age, were she to lose him.
Between a blurred sagacity
    That once had power to sound him,

And Love, that will not let him be
      The Judas that she found him,
Her pride assuages her almost,
As if it were alone the cost. –
He sees that he will not be lost,
      And waits and looks around him.

A sense of ocean and old trees.
      Envelops and allures him;
Tradition, touching all he sees,
      Beguiles and reassures him;
And all her doubts of what he says
Are dimmed with what she knows of days –
Till even prejudice delays
      And fades, and she secures him.

The falling leaf inaugurates
      The reign of her confusion;
The pounding wave reverberates
      The dirge of her illusion;
And home, where passion lived and died,
Becomes a place where she can hide,
While all the town and harbor side
      Vibrate with her seclusion.

We tell you, tapping on our brows,
      The story as it should be, --
As if the story of a house
      Were told, or ever could be;
We'll have no kindly veil between
Her visions and those we have seen, --
As if we guessed what hers have been,
      Or what they are or would be.

Meanwhile we do no harm; for they
      That with a god have striven,
Not hearing much of what we say,
      Take what the god has given;
Though like waves breaking it may be,
Or like a changed familiar tree,
Or like a stairway to the sea
      Where down the blind are driven.

Wowed by his dramatic performance, the class eagerly awaits another reading, but instead Pinsky announces his only commercial message for the day. He asks the students to log onto *favoritepoem.org.* "I guarantee viewing satisfaction and suggest that you contribute to keep the site going as revenue sources for the arts keeps drying up and lovers of poetry need to step up," he said.

It is time to hear the PLNU students' poetry. "Josh Morse, you're up." Pinsky steps aside and swings an arm toward the podium. With that, Josh begins reading his poem, "Goodness."

Goodness

It is his Grandmother's table in the mornings before noon.
I know the questions that can't be asked after she goes.
I enjoy my own curiosity because my ears love your generosity.
The presents of time, the presence of care.
The pursuit of goodness is a lifelong search. See.

The table is wooden and sits in the large kitchen
In the shaded neighborhoods of Arcadia where I was born.
You are at the sink, your untiring hands baking and washing themselves thin
Like the cookie sheet you pulled from the drawer.
And your cinnamon sugar smile is filling the room with the scent of welcome.

The table is again wooden, yet frayed and worn
In its new seat in Seal Beach where,
Though not shaded and not Arcadia,
Is warm with beach sun smiles and coastal eyes that you've pulled me into.

The table is glass now because the wooden one no longer fits,
Though I am no longer close to the kitchen,
I find you conveniently cleaning the vase closed to me
Pulled from the small cupboard of a smaller dining room.
Your voice is draping me in washed sheets and fresh-out-of-the-dryer shirts.
I am too comfortable to even consider the lack of kitchen we now have.
You have baked us into home with the oven that is in your chest

The glass table is now chipped around the edges
from a bump during its trip down the stairs
of the one-room apartment you and my grandfather had been renting.
I sit at this table, and you are in your bedroom, not quite asleep.

I sit at the chipped glass, waiting my turn to visit your bedside to thank you for the home,
before you move one last time and sit at the last great wooden table.

As soon as Josh finishes, Pinsky says, "Natalie Rosen, the mike is yours." Natalie reads:

Love Triangle

Kyoto. Dubai. Santiago. Budapest.
You pack the bags
I'll buy the tickets
Yes, I know we have no money.

Toronto. Capetown. Brisbane. Lima.
Let's start a travel jar
Save all our spare change
Oh, you want to purchase a new car?

Berlin. Nairobi. Bangkok. Tehran.
We'll make it work somehow
The world shall be our hoe
Wait, you just got promoted?

Athens. Cairo, Tokyo. Moscow.
Where you want to go, we'll go
You can save all your vacation days
You want to raise kids here at home?

Honolulu. St Louis. Portland, Orlando.
We'll travel within this country
Until our kids are old enough
What, you get airsick, carsick, seasick, and trainsick?

Los Angeles. Phoenix. Palm Springs. Chula Vista.
You never told me about that
But we've also never traveled together
… You want to marry me?

I never expected you to provide for me
I just wanted to be on a grade adventure together
I love traveling, but I love
You more. So my answer is yes.

As she finishes, Pinsky steps up. "Ellen Huang, your next."
Ellen reads:

You Might Not Be Struck by Lightning as You Wish

You might not be struck by the holy light,
jinxed by an angel,
implanted with surround sound of the heavens
and told what you need to do.
You might not find your
curled up fetal position,
jumbling twisted pretzel,
stressed out spaghetti monster –
all pulled apart and straightened out to be like others
as you wish.
You might not be tormented with the pleasurable torment
of a fiery match
(price tag says match made in heaven)
or an arrow piercing your heart
soon giving all that hangs over a place to rest –
At least not the same way.

But you will find yourself lightning unafraid
and loved so deeply that you cannot die.
Your hell and torment in love already spent, passionately,
      you'll discover a new bright season
underground as earth trembles.
You will feel a peace whirlwind you dance,
perhaps yet another thing others won't understand,
but your heart will reach your fingertips and stretch out through all your
ligaments,
Your soul the fire.
From here you can see the path to paradise is littered with celebration
colored with pride as it was originally created
And it won't what they jeer
how a hero should look, how a prince should lead
as you link hands, always beloved,
and spin right into His arms,
finally free.

When Ellen finishes, Pinsky thanks all three students and
offers a few general poetry writing guidelines. Ending his session
with a deep bow, he thanks everyone for their attendance.

The entire class simultaneously bolts upright, applauding widely as they send a wave of heartfelt gratitude in Pinsky's direction. I too am caught up in the moment, feeling truly honored to have spent a little secluded time with a renowned Poet Laureate.

Ellyn, Peggy and I have a few hours to relax before the next event, a stage performance of Pinsky, along with three PLNU music students who will add jazz vibes to his reading... shades of Jack Kerouac and David Amram (*Hummingbird Review*, Vol. 2, No. 1, Spring 2011) in Greenwich Village, mid-1950s.

Walking the grounds of PLNU on its Pacific Ocean front landscape is pure delight for me in contrast to my campus, a few city blocks of Camden, New Jersey, literally a few doors from where Walt Whitman lived and died. We dine in the student cafeteria, where the food is more than adequate with hot pizza, a crowd favorite, and ample offerings of greens and veggies, which ooze with goodness.

At 6:45 p.m., we enter the nearly filled, 375-seat auditorium, and sit in the rear right under the cameras of KCDS-TV, which videotapes and broadcasts the symposium events every year.

The houselights dim. Dean Nelson walks on stage and sets the table: "Ladies and gentleman, prepare for a fabulous evening of entertainment. It is my extreme pleasure to introduce our PLNU jazz trio, pianist Matthew Giles, bassist, Evan Killeen, and drummer, Steven Brown. Now please give a warm PLNU welcome to former U.S. Poet Laureate, Robert Pinsky."

Pinsky takes a sip of water and cozies up to the mike while patting his thigh as the jazz trio kicks into gear. The Poet Laureate bobs and weaves, keeping the beat as he opens his performance. He has memorized his poems and allows the music to capture an interlude, then pounces back as the musicians take their cue to soften. The performance reminded me of David Amram, who recalled his days in the Bowery circa 1957: "Jack Kerouac and I, along with Howard Hart and Philip Lamantia, pioneered the first ever jazz/poetry reading. Unbeknownst to us, it started a fad."[1]

Pinsky tells the audience that he and the musician have rehearsed except for the next poem, for which he invites the trio to play what they feel as he reads. The demonstration proves the marriage of music and poetry works well with *and* without a rehearsal.

The show ends all too soon. A standing ovation does not secure an encore this time. We exit the theatre in silence, recounting the day, thankful for the opportunity to walk in the shadow of a U.S. Poet Laureate for a day and evening, and especially grateful to Dr. Dean Nelson, and the hospitality of Point Loma Nazarene University students, faculty and staff.

1. Hummingbird Review Vol II No 1, spring 2011

PEGGY P. EDWARDS

ENGAGING THE POET

While teaching poetry writing to students at Point Loma Nazarene University as they overlooked the great Pacific, Robert Pinsky asked poets to raise their hands. He counted three student poets, but there were 120 students and teachers present, plus three guests from *The Hummingbird Review.* He proceeded to ask for questions from his audience:

Point Loma Nazarene University student: How did you start writing poetry?
    Robert Pinsky: I married young, a woman who after teaching middle school became a psychoanalyst. She is now Dr. Ellen Pinsky, and we've been married 52 years. She was my first inspiration. The point, though is (that) you can follow your intellectual passions at any time.
    PLNU: How do you get your inspiration?
    Pinsky: Art comes out of art. It's essential to keep an anthology with everything you love. Your anthology will feed your inspiration.
    PLNU: Why did you decide to come to Point Loma Nazarene University?
    Pinsky: I am resident poet at Stanford, so it's not too far to travel. Also, I have grandchildren in L.A., so from here, visiting them is a short distance. Also, I love to work with music.
    PLNU: Who was your inspiration as a student?
    Pinsky: Ivor Winters was my professor at Stanford. He uses wonderful imagery.
    PLNU: How would you advise us to write?
    Pinsky: Don't think about it as writing – think of it as speaking, how it sounds is what matters. I write poems anywhere and everywhere.
    PLNU: How did you develop your individual voice?
    Pinsky: Keep that anthology of your favorite things, your passions, what you most admire, what's important to you. Practice, perfect, work hard at it, cultivate your art.
    PLNU: How do you get around a writing block?

Pinsky: A block means something so daunting, frightening, is holding you back; you're running away from it. You have to overcome it. Take words, see them forwards, backwards and inside out, and everything related to them. Don't rush.

PLNU: How would you characterize your growth as a poet?

Pinsky: My goal is to do something great, not just be successful.

Pinsky then asked the three student poets to recite their work. As he did, he noted that he listens to technique, chops, rhythm, vowels and consonants – the sounds of the whole. He also said we should always donate to our favorite poetry project.

A student then asked Pinsky why he decided to focus on poetry rather than music. He answered that he tried music "but I sucked at it," so he decided to become a poet.

What a trip to get to listen to the Poet Laureate at one of our most beautiful campuses, nestled in the hills above the sea – the addition to music to his poetry was a nice treat. His teaching inspired me to keep an anthology and listen to the poetry of words.

DEAN NELSON

LOOKING AT TODAY FROM TEN YEARS PAST:
A CONVERSATION WITH VICENTE FOX

There is an antidote to Donald Trump's disheartening tweets about Mexico and Mexicans, and it comes from former Mexican President Vicente Fox. I'll leave it to readers to look up what Trump has tweeted about our neighbors, and what Fox has tweeted in response. The summary is that Trump thinks Mexicans are hurting the United States, and Fox's profane responses are the result of what he says is his Trump-induced Tourette's Syndrome. It's pretty entertaining, as far as politicians insulting each other go. But it's also so unnecessary, and not where the real substance from Fox resides.

What the exchanges remind me of, though, are the times I visited with Fox in 2011 to talk about Mexico's relationship with the U.S. The first conversation we had was in San Diego, and when we ran out of time, he suggested we continue the conversation at his ranch and presidential center in San Cristobal, Mexico. "We can have some real enchiladas there," he said, as if the thought of further discussion itself wasn't enough of an incentive.

A few months later, I spent a few days at Centro Fox, which is on a part of the land where his family had its broccoli farm. We had enchiladas in the same part of the house where he ate as a child.

The Fox Center, or Centro Fox, is a combination presidential library/community center/leadership institute, all on the property that has been his family's ranch for more than 100 years. The old walls from the historic cattle ranch are blended with modern architecture. His presidential papers are archived electronically for researchers, along with displays of significant events during his presidency, ornate saddles given to him by world leaders, replicas of his presidential office and cabinet meeting room, a gallery that exhibits local artists' work, open space for concerts and dance (Elton John and Carlos Santana appeared there for fundraisers), and banners from the ceiling with portraits of himself along with his heroes: Mahatma Gandhi, Nelson Mandela, Mother Teresa, Martin Luther King Jr., Lech Walesa, and Marie Curie.

Even though those conversations were in 2011, the points he made then are even more significant now. They can be summed up this way:

1) America needs immigrants.

2) A unified effort that combines Canada, the U.S. and Mexico is the only way to keep China from dominating the world economically.

3) A border wall is not only a waste of money, but it also won't make America safer. "Of course I am not for open borders," he told me. "I am for a regulated flow of migration."

4) The U.S. should either stop consuming drugs or legalize them.

I asked him how he evolved from being a corporate executive, where his sole purpose was to look out for himself and make more money, to a more outward-looking person who wanted to help those being crushed or ignored by corporations and governments.

He told me that it started with his 10-year college reunion.

His classmates had rented the University Club in Mexico City, one of the swankiest rooms in the city. They made sure the food was exquisite, the liquor plentiful, the cigars imported, and the women beautiful. They wanted to remember this reunion for one thing in particular: They wanted to impress each other. Some of the classmates were bankers, some were presidents of manufacturing companies, and some were CEOs. They were the nation's elite— including Fox. He was president of Coca-Cola in Mexico at the ripe young age of 32. It was a night for bragging. They had attended Iberoamericana University in Mexico City, a school run by the Jesuit Order of the Catholic Church, and they invited their main professor, Father Schiefler, to help them congratulate themselves.

Schiefler mingled with the newly enriched graduates as they preened in front of each other like so many peacocks, and then called for their attention. The classmates became quiet, in anticipation of the praise that would follow. What the priest said changed Fox forever.

"He thanked us for inviting him to the dinner and said he was pleased to be with us, but then he paused," Fox said. "He said, 'I feel very sad and sorrowful tonight. I think I failed in my teaching and my education with you. I tried to teach you to live for others and not for yourselves, to promote opportunities for others and not just enrich yourselves. I am disappointed. I am not going to stay for dinner with you. Good night.'"

Schiefler left the party, and the crowd stood in stunned silence. Fox said they felt ashamed of themselves and did the next best thing. "We all got drunk," he said.

But he got the message, and began thinking about what he had learned in college. He had studied Ignatius of Loyola, the founder of the Jesuits. He remembered that Ignatius was quite self-absorbed, much like Fox's graduating class. The Catholic Encyclopedia describes Ignatius as a man "affected and extravagant about his hair and dress, consumed with the desire of winning glory." At the age of 30, Ignatius was wounded in battle and, during a long, painful rehabilitation, had a spiritual revelation that propelled him into serving and educating others.

This began Fox's move from corporate ambition to political service.

Fox's 2007 autobiography goes deeper into that transformation. Some of his views published then seem even more timely now. They're also more thoughtful than what he's been posting lately on Twitter. Regarding the border wall:

"Walls don't work. The Great Wall of China didn't work. The Berlin Wall didn't work. The West Bank Barrier won't work. Walls *never* work. Walls are a medieval solution to a twenty-first-century problem. Mongols invade them. Escapees tunnel under them. Television beams over them. Palestinian car bombs explode them. Immigrants crawl through their barbed wire in the night, in search of a better life.

"Today... the United States isn't building a wall. It is building a prison. A wall of troops around the United States would suffocate the American dream. Inside the gilded cage of this new American hacienda envisioned by the isolationists, in a gated community surrounded by video cameras and guard dogs, the dream of the Americas would be forever hostage to fear, hate, greed and indifference....

"Now that Mexico is a democracy that puts computers in its schools and buys more products from the United States than all the greatest nations of Europe combined – a country with the rule of law, that retires its presidents to the farm to write books instead of letting them steal the silver – we should stop building walls between us and build a united continent instead." (pp. xviii-xiv)

Regarding tyrannical leaders:

"The dirty secret of the world's authoritarian regimes is this: They exist because we *let* them exist." (p. 122)

On globalism:

"The exciting part of globalism comes when you stop worrying about what you might lose alone and start thinking about what we might win together." (p. 212)

On immigration:

"Immigration is a no-win issue for politicians. Pro-reform Republicans circle warily around their conservative base in red states; Democrats do the same in blue states, where many working-class voters blame Mexicans for the loss of jobs. Today's leaders know what is morally right for people who are being treated as second-class citizens and what is economically best for America's future. The question is: Do they have the courage to stand up for what is right? Will they be guided by what Lincoln called 'the better angels of our nature'?

"No cause is closer to God's will than the spiritual imperative that we love all people, treat others as we would be treated, and give every human being equal rights and equal dignity." (p. 349)

On the politics of fear:

"Will the First World ever be safe if the only citizens who matter are those born inside its walls?" (p. 350)

"The irony, of course, is that walls of fear don't protect the poor, the rich, or the middle class – *they just keep us apart*, so that those with jobs to give can't offer them to the poor who need them. The razor wire at the guarded border, the government agent tapping your phones – these do not protect you from any threat. They *are* the threat. There are no walls high enough and no soldiers vigilant enough to keep out the poor, to jam the transmission of new ideas, to deny the hopes of people willing to work for a better life…. Contrary to the words of Robert Frost, good fences do not always make good neighbors. In a global economy, the best way to build a clean, prosperous neighborhood in our hemisphere is to help the neighbors to build a better house next door." (p. 351)

On the future of America:

Quoting de Tocqueville, who marveled at the prosperity, opportunity and human values he found in America, "America is great because it is good," the French writer said. "If America ever ceases to be good, America will cease to be great."

Fox followed up that quote with: "This is brand U.S.A.: the goodness of America. And the day America no longer stands for this goodness – the day the United States turns out the torch on the Statue of Liberty and replaces it with the searchlight of the guard tower, the day that the visionary America of the Marshall Plan becomes the Fortress America of the Minutemen – on that day America will cease to be good and will no longer be great." (p. 352)

I had to read that last line again and marvel at the timing. In an era where the effort is in trying to make America great again, there's the recipe right there in Fox's book, not in a tweet.

We can be great when we focus on making each other great. It's what Xavier learned, what Fox learned from his college professor, and what we can all learn again.

TWO LANGUAGES, NO WALL, MANY VOICES
POETRY

Curated and Translated By
PEGGY P. EDWARDS

PEGGY P. EDWARDS

Bienvenidos a "Dos Lenguajes, Sin Paredes, Muchas Voces," nuestra colección especial de poemas, poetas y cuentos que celebran las culturas hispanas y latinas, y nuestra relación inquebrantable con ellas. Hemos seleccionado una docena de poemas de todas partes del mundo hispanoparlante, la mayoría del siglo 19, pero otros de mucho antes.

Voces poeticas de diez paises -- México, España, Cuba, Puerto Rico, Argentina, Colombia, Perú, Ecuador, Venezuela, y los Estados Unidos -- comprobante de que el sentimiento poetico vive en todas partes, siempre. Terminamos con un obsequio especial, la corta pero vital amistad entre los gigantes literarios, Pablo Neruda de Chile y Federico García Lorca de España.

Tambien incluímos piezas del libro "Lalalandia" escrito por Peggy P. Edwards además del libro "Cuentos del Pueblo", también publicado por the Village Publishing Club de Laguna Woods. Creció bilingüe, maestra de lenguaje por vida, Peggy es nuestra interprete en esta jornada.

Welcome to "Two Languages, No Wall, Many Voices," our special collection of poems, poets and stories celebrating the Hispanic and Latin cultures and our long, special relationship with them — and they with each other. We have selected a dozen poems from all over the Spanish-speaking world, mostly from the 19th century, but stretching as far back as 1520.

Poetic voices from ten nations — Mexico, Spain, Cuba, Puerto Rico, Argentina, Colombia, Peru, Ecuador, Venezuela and the United States – offer standing proof that poetic sentiment lives everywhere, forever. We finish with quite a treat, the short-lasting but vital friendship between literary giants, Pablo Neruda of Chile and Federico García Lorca of Spain.

Also included are pieces by Peggy P. Edwards from her book *Lalalandia*, as well as *Village Stories,* published by the Publishing Club of Laguna Woods Village. Raised bilingual and a lifelong language teacher, Peggy serves as our bilingual interpreter on this journey.

MANUEL ACUÑA • MEXICO

A UNA FLOR

Cuando tu broche apenas se entreabría
Para aspirar la dicha y el contento
¿Te doblas ya y cansada y sin aliento,
Te entregas al dolor y a la agonía?

¿No ves, acaso, que esa sombra impía
Que ennegrece el azul del firmamento
Nube es tan sólo que al soplar el viento,
Te dejará de nuevo ver el día?

¡Resucita y levántate!...Aun no llega
La hora de que en el fondo de tu broche
Des cabida al pesar que te doblega.

Injusto que para el sol es tu reproche,
Que esa sombra que pasa y que te ciega,
Es una sombra, pero aún no es la noche.

TO A FLOWER

When your bud barely half-opens
To breathe happiness and contentment
You double over, tired, breathless,
You give into pain and agony?

Can't you see that perhaps that vile shadow
That darkens the blue of the firmament
Is no more than a cloud that when blown by a breeze will let you see
the day anew?

Arise and lift yourself ..The time has not yet come when at the root
of your bud
You'll yield to the pain that blows you over.

Not fair that you blame the sun,
The shadow which passes and blinds you,
Is a shadow, but not yet night.

Written in 1849

ANDRES BELLO • VENEZUELA

RUBIA

¿Sabes, rubia, qué gracia solicito
cuando de ofrendas cubro los altares?
No ricos muebles, no soberbios lares,
ni una mesa que adule el apetito.

De Aragua a las orillas un distrito
que me tribute fáciles manjares,
do vecino a mis rústicos hogares
entre peñascos corra un arroyito.

Para acogerme en el calor estivo,
que tenga una arboleda también quiero,
do crezca junto al sauce el coco altivo.

¡Feliz yo si en este albergue muero;
y al exhalar mi aliento fugitivo,
sello en tus labios el adiós postrero!

BLONDE

Do you know blonde the grace I pray for
what altars I cover with my offerings?
Not luxury, nor superb lands,
neither a table to satisfy my appetite.

At the edge of Aragua a place
that grants me simple pleasures,
where close to my rustic home
 among rocks runs a rivulet.

Where summer warms me,
and also where an orchard grows
where the willow grows by the proud coconut.

I would die happy in this refuge;
and as I draw my fleeting breath,
I seal on your lips a goodbye kiss.

Written in 1781

JUANA BORRERO • CUBA

CREPUSCULAR

Todo es quietud y paz…en la penumbra
se respira el olor de los jazmines,
y, más allá, sobre el cristal del río,
se escucha el aleteo de los cisnes

que como grupo de nevadas flores,
resbalan por la tersa superficie.
Los oscuros murciélagos resurgen
de sus mil ignorados escondites,

y vueltas mil, y caprichosos giros
por la tranquila atmósfera describen;
o vuelan luego rastreando el suelo,

rozando apenas con su alas grises
del agrio cardo el amarillo pétalo,
de humilde malva la corola virgen.

TWILIGHT

All is peace and quiet in the twilight
one breathes the jasmine fragrance,
and, farther away, over the river crystal
one hears the flapping wings of swans

who like flowers made of snow
slide through the frozen surface.
The dark bloodsucker bats emerge
from their one thousand ignored hideouts.

and twirl and turn one thousand times
through the quiet atmosphere describe;
or drag their wings on the floor below,

their sharp grey wings barely touch the yellow petal of the bitter
thistle,
the humble salve of the virgin corolla.

Written in 1877

GUTIERRE DE CETINA • SPAIN

ENTRE ARMAS

Entre armas, guerra, fuego, ira y furores
que el soberbio francés tienen opreso,
cuando al aire es más turbio y más espeso,
allí me aprieta el fiero ardor de amores.

Miro al cielo, los árboles, las flores,
y en ellos hallo mi dolor expreso;
que en el tiempo más frío y más avieso
nacen y reverdecen mis temores.

Digo llorando, "¡Oh dulce primavera! ¿Cuándo será que a mi
esperanza vea,
verde, prestar al alma algún sosiego?"

Mas temo que mi fin mi suerte fiera
tan lejos de mi bien quiere que sea
entre guerra y furor, ira, armas, fuego.

AMONG ARMS

Among arms, war, fire, fury and ire
 arrogantly oppressed by the French,
when the air is turbulent and thicker,
there I'm pierced by the fiery ardor of love.

I see the sky, the trees, the flowers,
and in them I find my pain expressed;
that in the coldest, darkest times
are born anew and my fears with them.

Crying I say, "Oh sweet spring!
When will it be that I see hope anew
 green, loan my soul some peace?

I fear more that my end be fierce
so far away from my good and wants to be
among war and fury, ire, arms and fire.

Written in 1520

RUBÉN DARIO • NICARAGUA

LO FATAL

Dichoso el árbol que es apenas sensitivo.
y más la piedra dura porque esa ya no siente,
pues no hay dolor más grande que el dolor de ser vivo
ni mayor pesadumbre que la vida consciente.

Ser, y no saber nada, y ser sin rumbo cierto,
y el temor de haber sido y un futuro terror…
y el espanto seguro de estar mañana muerto,
y sufrir por la vida y por la sombra y por

lo que no conocemos y apenas sospechamos,
y la carne que tienta con sus frescos racimos,
y la tumba que aguarda con sus fúnebres ramos,
¡ y no saber adónde vamos,
ni de dónde venimos!...

THE DEADLY

Fortunate the tree that is barely sensitive,
and even more the hard rock because it no longer feels,
there is no greater pain than that of being alive
nor greater hardship than conscious life.
To be and not know anything, without real direction,
and the fear of having been and a future terror...
the certainty of death tomorrow,
and to suffer for life and for the shadow and for
what is unknown and what we barely suspect,
and flesh which tempts with its fresh bounty,
and the tomb awaiting with its morbid bouquets,
and not know where we are going and from where we came!

Written in 1867

SALVADOR DE MADRIAGA • SPAIN

ARDIENTE CORAZON

Ardiente corazón, alma serena,
Fuego es luz que en tus pupilas vibra
Pero en la luz el fuego se equilibra
Y de radiante paz tu pecho llena.

De la amargura de tu larga pena.
Por alquimia sútil tu alma se libra,
Destilando en su más secreta fibra
La dulzura de amor que en tu voz suena.

Las lágrimas que viertes hacia dentro
Riegan este rosal – rosas y espinas –
Que florecen en tu boca sonriente.

Todo lo que penetra hasta tu centro
Lo elevas, transfiguras e iluminas,
Alma serena, corazón ardiente.

PASSIONATE HEART

Passionate heart, serene soul,
fire is the light that in your pupils tremble,
But in the light the fire is balanced
and fills your chest with radiant peace.

From long-lasting bitterness
You free your soul by alchemy
Distilling its most subtle fiber
Love's sweet sound is heard in your voice.

The tears you shed inward
Water this rosebush – roses and thorns –
Which then blossom on your smiling mouth.

All that penetrates your inner center
You elevate, transfigure and illuminate,
Serene soul, passionate heart.

Written in 1886

LOLA RODRIGUEZ DE TIO • PUERTO RICO

LAS HORAS

¡Qué alegres son las horas! Cual bandada
De palomas que vagan por el cielo
Y rasgan de la aurora el tenue velo
Que abrillanta la luz tornasolada.

Así cruzan la atmósfera azulada,
En ruidoso tropel con manso vuelo,
Trayendo una ilusión, un nuevo anhelo,
A mi musa feliz y enamorada.

Yo las siento pasar, por mi fortuna,
Como rayos purísimos de luna
Que bañan mis ensueños dulcemente;

Y mi hora postrera sólo ansío
Que llegue lo más tarde al hogar mío,
Donde tiene el amor culto ferviente.

THE HOURS

How joyful are the hours! Like a flock
Of doves that wander through the sky
And tear off the tenuous veil from daybreak
Brightening the iridescent light.

Thus they cross the blued atmosphere,
In a raucous bustle in peaceful flight,
Bringing an illusion, a new desire,
To my happy loving muse.

I feel them pass, luckily for me,
As pure rays of moonlight
That sweetly bathe my fantasies;

And my last hour I only desire
Comes very late to my home,
Where a cult of love has a fervent altar.

Written in 1843

PEGGY P. EDWARDS • MEXICO/USA

EL AGUA ES MI ELEMENTO

El agua es mi elemento,
El agua es donde casi vuelo
Hasta el cielo!
El agua es mi elemento,
Giro y taconeo
Quince veces los talones.
Floto sobre mi espalda,
Luego giro de cada lado…
Luego giro al revés.
Si yo pudiera…
Me quedaría aquí todo
El santo día y toda la divina noche.
Es suave…
Como seda…
Ondea con mi cada movimiento,
Me salpica – me canta – me silba.
Me corre por la nariz, oídos, y por la boca,
Me cosquilla los dedos de los pies.
Me calienta y me llena de éxtasis,
¡Soy yo! ¡Soy libre!
Me deja ser quien soy…
El agua es mi elemento.

WATER IS MY ELEMENT

Water is my element,
Water is where I almost fly
Into the sky!
Water is my element,
I pirouette,
And click my heels 15 times.
I float on my back,
Then flip to each side…
Then into a backwards summersault.
If I could…
I would stay all this saintly day
And into the divine night.
It's soft…
It's smooth …
It ripples with pleasure at my every move,
It splashes – it sings – it whistles…
It runs up my nose, my ears, and into my mouth,
It tickles my toes,
It warms me and fills me with ecstasy,
I'm me! I'm free!
It lets me be me…
Water is my element.

Written in 2017

DIEGO FERNANDEZ ESPIRO • SPAIN

BOHEMIO

Nació para triunfar, y la victoria
desdeñó con estoica altanería.
Fue su existencia una ruidosa orgía,
y un largo sueño su perdida historia.

Nostálgico del arte y de la gloria,
cuyo sublime vértigo sentía,
deshojó con sarcástica alegría
el laurel prometido en su memoria.

Su noble corazón se hizo pedazos
al golpe rudo de su horrible suerte.
Y rotos ya los terrenales lazos.

De su brillante juventud cansada,
hundiéndose en la noche de la muerte,
huyó del mundo y se perdió en la nada.

BOHEMIAN

He was born to triumph, and victory
he scorned with stoical arrogance.
His existence was a noisy orgy,
and a long dream his lost history.

Lonely for art and its glory,
whose sublime vertigo he felt,
with sarcastic happiness he tore off
 leaves of his memory's promised laurel.

His noble heart fell to pieces
At the rude crash of his horrible fate.
His earthly ties now broken.

Of his brilliant, tired youth,
Sinking in the night at death,
He fled from the world lost in nothingness.

Written in 1872

JULIO FLOREZ • COLOMBIA

CANDOR

Azul...azul...azul estaba el cielo.
El hálito quemaste del estío.
Comenzaba a dorar el terciopelo
del prado, en donde se remansa el río.

A lo lejos, el humo de un bohío,
tal de una novia el intocado velo,
se alza hasta perderse en el vacío
con un ondulante y silencioso vuelo.

De pronto me dijiste: "El amor mío
es puro y blando, así como ese río
que rueda allá sobre el lejano suelo."

y me miraste al terminar, tranquila,
con el alma asomada a tu pupila.
Y estaba azul tu alma como el cielo.

CANDOR

Blue…blue…blue was the sky.
You burned the halo from the coming summer.
The browning of the velvet prairie had begun where the river is
pooled.

In the distance, the smoke of a chimney,
like that of an untouched bride's veil,
lifts itself until it's lost in the emptiness
with an undulating and silent flight.

Suddenly you said to me: "My love
is pure and soft, like the river
that rolls over there beyond the distant earth."

And then you looked at me, serenely,
your soul showing through your pupils.
And your soul was as blue as the sky.

Written in 1867

LYDIA MASCARIN • USA

GAVIOTAS

El mar profundo
Viento de lluvia torrencial,
Gaviotas que vuelan con alas rotas
Se pierden en las nubes de siempre,
Llegando al puerto casi secas,
Con sus plumas aceitadas
Pues es lo que Dios les dio
Para poder continuar,
Descansan en enramadas y lagunas de silencio.
La mañana llega con el sol
Iluminando el día,
El murmullo de pájaros saliendo
De sus nidos
Los barcos pesqueros regresan,
Las gaviotas vuelan a sus lados pidiendo
No hay para todas.
Regresan al mar,
Uno puede oír el aleteo de sus
Alas,
Volando, volando, volando.

SEAGULLS FLIGHT

The profound sea
Winds of torrential rain,
Seagulls flying with torn wings
Lose themselves through clouds of always.
Arriving at the harbor partially dried,
With their oiled feathers
For that's what God gave them
So that they can continue,
Resting in bushes and lagoons of silence,
Morning arrives with the sun
Illuminating the day,
The murmur of birds coming
Out of their nests,
Fishing boats return,
Seagulls fly to their sides begging,
There's not enough to feed all.
Once more they go out to sea,
One can hear the fluttering of
Wings,
Fly, fly, fly.

Written in 2017

ELLYN MAYBE • USA

ALGÚN DÍA NUESTRA PAZ VENDRÁ

un día cayó la poesía del cielo
y los animales crecieron colas de pentámetro yámbico
y la gente respiró estrellas

un día música cayó del cielo
y la arquitectura se volvió simfónica
y la gente respiró harmonía

un día memoria cayó del cielo
y el pasado, presente y futuro se espolvoreó como harina
y la gente respiró asombro

humo y ceniza
tan distantes como los dos lados de la misma moneda

SOME DAY OUR PEACE WILL COME

one day poetry dropped from the sky
and the animals grew iambic pentameter tails
and the people breathed in stars

one day music dropped from the sky
and the architecture turned symphonic
and the people breathed in harmony

one day memory dropped from the sky
and the past present and future sifted like flour
and the people breathed wonder

smoke and ash
as distant as two sides of the same coin

JOSE ASUNCION SILVA • COLUMBIA

SUSPIRO

Si en tus recuerdos ves algún día
entre la niebla de lo pasado
surgir la triste memoria mía
medio borrada ya por los años,

piensa que fuiste siempre mi anhelo
y si el recuerdo de amor tan santo
mueve tu pecho; nubla tu cielo.
llena de lágrimas tus ojos garzos;

¡ah! no me busques aquí en la tierra
donde he vivido, donde he luchado,
sino en el reino de los sepulcros
donde se encuentran paz y descanso.

YEARNING

If among your memories someday you see
in the past fog
arise my sad memory
half erased by the passing years.

consider that you were always my desire
and if the memory of such a saintly love
moves your breast; clouds your sky.
fills your beautiful eyes with tears;

Oh! Don't look for me here on earth
where I have lived, where I have fought,
but rather in the empire of tombstones
where peace and rest are found.

Written in 1865

ABRAHAM VALDELOMAR • PERU

TRISTEZA

Mi infancia, que fue dulce, serena, triste y sola,
se deslizó en la paz de una aldea lejana
entre el manso rumor con que muere una ola
y el tañer doloroso de una vieja campana.

Dábame el mar la nota de su melancolía;
el cielo, la serena quietud de su belleza;
los besos de mi madre, una dulce alegría,
y la muerte del sol, una vaga tristeza.

En la mañana azul, al despertar, sentía
el canto de las olas como una melodía
y luego el soplo denso, perfumado, del mar,

y lo que él me dijera, aun en mi alma persiste;
mi padre era callado y mi madre era triste
y la alegría nadie me la supo enseñar.

SADNESS

My childhood, which was sweet, serene, sad and lonely
took place in the peace of a faraway village
between the tame murmur of a dying wave
and the painful tolling of an old bell.

The sea gave me its melancholic note,
the sky, the serene quietude of its beauty;
my mother's kisses, a sweet gladness,
and the sun's death, a vague sadness.

Upon awakening to the blue morning, I felt
the waves' song like a melody
and then the perfumed sea's dense breeze,

and what he told me still persists in my soul;
my father was quiet and my mother was sad
and of happiness no one could show me.

Written in 1888

FELIX VALENCIA • ECUADOR

LA GRAN MENTIRA

Cristo y Judas son flores de heroísmo
y la una sombra agranda la otra lumbre;
si Cristo es grande como toda cumbre,
Judas es negro como todo abismo.

Mas los dos, por extraño fatalismo,
al predicar amor y mansedumbre,
el uno es presa de ebria muchedumbre,
el otro es un verdugo de si mismo.

Mientras tanto el Dios hombre y el suicida,
hasta hoy no pueden con sus muertes rudas
disminuir las miserias de la vida.

¡Y entre tantos horrores no se ha visto
un acto más infame que el de Judas
ni un morir más inútil que el de Cristo!

THE GREAT LIE

Christ and Judas are fruits of heroism
one's shadow enlarges the other's fire;
if Christ is great as all height,
Judas is black as all abyss.

Yet both, by strange fatality,
upon predicting love and gentleness,
the one is the prisoner of the drunken mass,
the other his own executioner.

Meanwhile the man God and the suicide,
are not able, with their crude deaths,
to lessen life's miseries

And among so many horrors, there remains no more infamous act
than Judas'
Nor a death more useless that Christ's!

Written in 1886

IRVING BERLIN • USA

ALWAYS/SIEMPRE

F / fa
I'll be loving you, Always.
Yo te amaré, Siempre.
C7   *F*
With a love that's true…Always
Yo te voy a amar…Siempre
F
When the things you've planned
Cuando te va mal
A
Need a helping hand.
Allí yo voy a estar.
E7   A   C7
I will understand… Always…Always
Yo voy a entender…Siempre…Siempre

F   F7
Days may not be fair…Always
Vas a mejorar…   Siempre
D7   Cm Gm
That's when I'll be there…Always
Allí yo voy a estar …   Siempre
Gm   Bm6
Not for just an hour

No por una hora
F   G7
Not for just a day
Solo por un dia
C7   F
Not for just a year but ALWAYS.
Solo por un año pero SIEMPRE.

Written in 1925

TWO LANGUAGES, ONE WALL, MANY VOICES
PROSE

PEGGY P. EDWARDS

LA MUSICA

Fueron los tiempos peores cuando Solasi Doremi salvó a Lalalandia con música.

Durante esos días tan duros la gente ya no escuchaba la música. A causa de bombas, batallas y balas ya no escuchaban nada. La música estaba ahora apagada. Sin opera, valses, salsa, bachata, y romances dejó de existir el amor. Vivían escondidos en los restos de sus casas. Guardaban silencio – apagaron la música.

Pero Solasi Doremi era diferente; ella era divergente. Amaba la música y nadie podría pararla. La tocaba calladita y hasta componía bellas melodías. Ella
siguió cantando, bailando y tocando su música (Aunque la dejó su mejor amigo y estaba muy solita), ella siguió con su música – si no se moriría.

Lalalandia, para entonces, por el odio y el miedo había sido vencida; la música censurada de lejos y cercana. Pero Solasi Doremi tocó su dulce cuatro, su instrumento favorito; tocó la guitarra, el violín, y los tambores. El piano sintió sus dulces dedos bailar ballet sobre sus teclas. Cuando dormía soñaba en música, amor y romance.

Pero estaba muy enferma la gente de Lalalandia; se morían y ya no resistían. "¿De qué vale la vida?" Dijo un viejo a su vieja, "Escucha palpitar las pocas notas que quedan en tu corazón, es ya demasiado tarde, no hay remedio, no hay más música, ya es el tiempo de decirnos adiós."

Los viejos y jóvenes ahora lo mismo sentían, todos llenos de odio y de amargura; todos se rendían y juntos se morían.

Menos Solasi Doremi, ella era diferente, era divergente; ella siguió tocando su música.

Ella, poco antes de que fuera demasiado tarde, voló de su jaula, "Es hoy o es nunca," dijo. Y entro a la guerra de afuera. Sin importarle lo turbio, las balas y bombas, se paró en la luz de sol y comenzó a cantar. Tocó y cantó "Siempre / *Always*", su canción preferida. Como por milagro, toda la gente buena y sencilla que quedaba, no sólo oía, pero también con ella cantaba.

Pero los malos y amargados; los que adoraban el odio no oyeron nada – sí se fijaron que la gente buena y sencilla había cambiado y exigieron escucharan su mensaje de odio. Un odioso baboso tiró una piedra que le dio a Solasi en medio de la frente.

Pero a Solasi Doremi nadie la paraba; siguió tocando su música. Ahora toda la gente buena y decente paró lo que hacía; soltaron el odio y la amargura, y se fueron alegrando con la música. Fue entonces cuando bailando, tocando y cantando regresó su mejor amigo – y toda la gente buena y decente – los que amaban la música – a bailar, y cantar se juntaron. La vieja y su viejo exhalaron, y con gran gratitud exclamaron, "Este es el día que Lalalandia despertó a la música – no todo está perdido, hemos ganado. Bravo Solasi Doremi y su maravillosa música.

Hoy los grandes y chicos, todas las razas, géneros y colores, todos cantan "Siempre / *Always*" juntos. Y cuando la gente recuerda los tiempos más oscuros comienza de nuevo a cantar y bailar su música.

THE MUSICIAN

It was the darkest of times when Solati Doremi saved Lalalandia with Music.

These were the worst times; people no longer listened to music. The bombing and shooting had taken their hearing. They no longer were interested in music at all. No opera, fox trots and waltzes, salsa and romances were all part of the past now, and love quite forgotten. People lived hidden in what was left of their houses. They had to keep quiet – no music at all.

Solati Doremi though was different; she was divergent. She loved music and couldn't be stopped. She played oh so quietly and even composed lovely love songs. She just went right on singing, dancing and playing her music (Never mind that her BFF had fled and she was now quite alone), she went on playing the music – it kept her from dying.

Lalalandia by then had surrendered to the hate and the fear; all music was banned from afar and up near. But Solati Doremi stroked her sweet ukulele, her dear little pet; she strummed her guitar and beat on her drums. The piano felt her solace as her fingers danced ballet on its keys. When she could sleep, she dreamed in Music, Love and Romance.

But the people of Lalalandia were sick; they were dying; they were all giving up. "No use to go on living", said an old man to his old woman, "Listen to the last beating of your poor old thumping heart, it's too late, no more music now's the time to let go, time for good bye."

The young and the old now had something in common; they were all sick with their hate; they were all giving up; together they were dying.

Except for Solati Doremi, she was different, divergent; she went right on playing her music.

Just before it was too late, she flew out of her cage, "it's today or it's never," she said. She stepped out into the war; out to the streets. In spite of the racket, the battles, bullets and bombs, she stood in the sunshine – and started singing her songs. She played and she sang "Always/*Siempre*" her favorite song. Somehow and miraculously, all the good and decent people who were left could not only hear her, but joined in her song.

But the stupid and mean ones; the lovers of hate heard nothing at all -- they noticed a change in the good and decent people and demanded they listen to their message of hatred. A mean, ignorant moron threw a big rock that hit Solati Doremi in the middle of her forehead.

But Solati Doremi could never be stopped; she went right on playing her music. Now all the good and the decent stopped what they were doing, they let go of the hate and basked in the music. Just then her BFF came back waltzin', dancin' and romancing; and so all the good and decent people – the lovers of music -- joined in the dancing and started to sing. The Old Man and Old Woman breathed a great sigh of relief, and said, "This is the day Lalalandia finally awakened to music – all is not lost. Hurrah for Solati Doremi and the Music."

Today the young and the old, all races, genders and colors, we all sing "Always / *Siempre*" together. And when people remember the darkest of times, they start singing their Music.

ISAAC LOMELI

FROM *THE UNEXAMINED LIFE OF A BROWN MAN*

Introduction

If you had gone to my blog in its infancy, the subtitle would have read, "In a nation where the White voice is ubiquitous and the Black voice a squeaky wheel, I offer some noise from the otherwise silent or unheard Chicano voice." If I had to rename this collection it would probably be, *Voices.* The stories that follow are pictures of the world through my eyes. These eyes of mine see things from a Brown man's standpoint.

The unexamined life of the Brown man isn't only about showing non-brown people what's going on, but to Brown people as well. Us Brown people live our life without giving much thought to it being a story that teaches us who we are. There are not many books we have read about people like ourselves. There are not many movies, or TV shows, that tell our side of the story. The only two books I read in high school that weren't assigned to me were about black folks. So, as a writer today, I try to give people like me a place to go to discover identity, to help define it, to bring hope, and to bring the joy of storytelling.

To the Chicano, Mexican, Mexican-American, and/or Latino who I represent, I can only hope that I get it right for you. I hope I bring back fond memories and make you say, "Primo, I couldn't have said it any better myself." For everyone else, I welcome you into my mind. *Mi casa es su casa.* I only ask that you listen. That you enjoy. That you learn. This is the world that has been unexamined. Allow me to examine it for you all.

When I first began to write, my stories involved a character like myself bringing his fantasies to life. I grew up in your average difficult ghetto, writing to escape my reality. In my early stories, adventure and action were key. My characters were confident and cool, unlike me.

My stories today are about making my reality come true; not my fantasies. These stories you're about to read are compelling. My characters are broken, but not without hope.

In my early days, I did not want to examine my own life. I spent my free time thinking of living a better life, which meant having money and nice things and living in a house in a nice neighborhood. Today, all I do is examine my life from cover to cover. It is this personal examination of myself that brings you these stories. These stories for myself are intended to make my life matter, and everything negative to have some meaning to it. I have learned that no matter how tragic my life's events are, they will never be without a good reason, or in vain; at the very least, that reason will always be to share it with you. My life, in all of its pain and suffering and failures and letdowns, is still worth living. It is the unexamined life that isn't worth living. For when we examine the life of another, we examine our own lives in relation to that and it teaches us something deeper about ourselves. The one great thing it can lead to is empathy for each other.

Empathy is the cure for hatred, and all things awful in this country. Empathy causes us to seek first to understand and then to be understood. It teaches us that we are not always right, that we don't see things the way they are, but how we are. It teaches us humanity and humility. It teaches us to share. I'm sharing my story, my life, in order that I don't have to struggle alone. I am asking you to struggle with me as I will struggle with you; and we will rejoice together when we make it through.

My life will no longer be unexamined. Enjoy.

Part I: Examining My Childhood

(The following are stories about me, my family and friends. Some names have been changed.)

The Eastside

All the streets are long and wide and end at the wall that separates us from the other side. You have to be home before the streetlights come on—that's the rule out here—but half the time they stay off. These streets are dark, and mine is darker than most.

This is my story, so to me it's darker, yet dearer. This is the Eastside…the other side of the tracks…the place *some* drive by, not stop by.

85

I've grown up here. It wasn't always this way. It used to be a decent neighborhood. I used to play in these streets. Now, I stay away from these streets. It's the eastside, so you know we got eastside problems: gangs, drugs, *Mexicans,* a liquor store, a park with more violence than play and more crying than laughing, and no pleasure without pain.

People don't walk these streets, they lurk…yup, lurk. I'm not in a gang—don't want to be—and I don't do drugs; but I am Mexican—whether I like it or not. It seems I'm always on the receiving end of violence. I guess it doesn't pay to be Mr. Nice-guy in my barrio.

Speaking of violence, let me tell you about how I got here— on the Eastside.

It was the 70's and I was five. Like most Mexicans in those days you went where there were jobs. The city was a good place to find them. You see I grew up on a ranch with my grandparents—my mother was a child herself when she had me, so she took some time off from mothering until she was old enough to be a mother.

My grampa' worked on this ranch from morning to evening, while my grama' would work in the town we lived in—she worked taking care of old folks. Well, my mom finally decided she wanted to be a mother and take my new baby brother and me to the Valley where my new dad lived—I never did call my brother's dad, dad, he was just Fred to me.

Now how did violence bring me here? One night we were living some place, and my Dad came home covered in blood. The next thing I knew we were in Anaheim, CA, home of Disneyland, the happiest place on Earth.

It was in a new city and the apartments we moved into were fairly new. I had never seen new buildings before, with new paint and new carpet, and new streets and sidewalks, and new trees. It sure was beautiful.

Everything is beautiful when it's new. I was new…my baby brother was newer…the 70's were newer to the beginning of time than today. So begins my new story…from a new voice. This is a new time and the Eastside is where new beginnings take place.

Disneyland

I know, I know. What an amazing place to live, down the street from Disneyland. For as long as I can remember I knew who Mickey Mouse was. I knew all about the Mickey Mouse Club—about Goofy, and Mini, Donald, and Pluto. I would sit in front of the TV at my grandmother's ranch and sing like every other American kid, M-I-C-K-E-Y-M-O-U-S-E. And, it brought joy to my young heart.

Like every other kid it was my dream to one day go to Disneyland and shake hands with Mickey Mouse. I would never have thought that I would be living a stone's throw away…and, I would have never thought it would bring me so much pain, fear, and sadness.

In this moment life looked like a fairytale. On one side of me was Disneyland and on the other, The Big A—home of the California Angels. Sandwiched between two dreams like peanut butter and jelly. I was a little boy who felt like everything was possible.

At one point in my life baseball was my favorite sport, back when everyone played it *for the love of the game.* Imagine being squeezed between two of your wildest dreams. Now, before you think how wonderful it would be, imagine the pressure. At the same time it was a dream it would soon become a reminder of everything that was just out of my reach.

Baseball aside—until another time—and about that fear. It was probably our first night in our new apartment. We were all quietly asleep well before 9:30pm. We were all nestled in bed with thoughts of Disneyland in our head. Our pictures newly hung on the wall of our new apartment, not a creature was stirring…not even Mickey Mouse.

When all of a sudden came a boom and a bang. My parents, like plastic army men on their stomachs, low crawled to the living room windows.

"GET BACK!!! Stay in your room." They warned.

My little brother and I squeezed each other tight. Again, the sounds grew louder and stronger. I was the oldest so I shielded him with my body and did my best to be brave in front of him. It sounded like bombs exploding in our courtyard. We laid there afraid waiting for Momma and Daddy to tell us all was ok. But all we heard were more explosions.

Finally after what seemed like an eternity our parents began to scream.

"Kids…Isaac, Shorty…come look."

We looked at each other and were too scared to move. And then again my parents screamed, "Come. Look." And again we were frozen with fear. Then we heard, "Hurry…you're gonna miss it."

Now for whatever reason the words, you're gonna miss it, got us up out of bed and running out the door—I guess kids just don't like to miss a thing. As we approached the front door I could see the other neighbors all out looking up.

It was an amazing sight. Big bright colorful lights filled the sky. I didn't know what I was looking at until my mother said, "Come, look at the fireworks." Wow, so this was fireworks. It was the most amazing thing my young eyes had seen.

For the first several years, fireworks were the greatest thing in my life. I never missed them, and I always begged my mom to let us stay up until the fireworks came on. But, as you can imagine this fascination lost its shine.

Today when others look at the sky to enjoy the fourth of July, I merely glance occasionally, and focus more on the people looking at the fireworks. It's a reminder of wonder and amazement. If you ever want to see what it looks like just look at all those faces, young and old, watching those fireworks light the sky fantastic. Everything is beautiful when it's new.

E-Tickets

You always knew it was summer again. Back in that day firework season only lasted from Cinco de Mayo till Labor day. Fireworks meant summer was on its way.

Even back in the day Disneyland was a treat—even though we lived less than a mile away our pocketbooks kept us miles apart—and what a treat it was when Leroy's mother took us all to Disneyland for his 8th birthday. It was the greatest birthday ever—come on, your mother takes you and your best friends to Disneyland for your birthday, what possibly could be done to outdo that party?

It was Raymond, my brother Max, and myself. We woke up that morning with so much energy it literally felt like my insides were going to explode. There was this rush that I had never felt before. I just remember being so full of joy and anxiety. I couldn't wait to see it all with my very own eyes.

Now this wasn't the first time I had been, but it was the first time I was going with friends. It was the first time we were going with our own game plan. It was the first time going where we were in control of what we did and didn't do, what we ate and didn't eat, and roamed where we wanted to roam. It was a beautiful thing.

It started off the happiest place on earth. Until it was time to go on the big rides. That is when my joy turned to fear. The ride was Space Mountain. I had never been big enough to get on the ride before, but now I was. It was time to meet my demon. All my fears came to this crossroads. Would I take it on with bravery and honor, or would I cower and cry away.

I'd like to tell a story of bravery and courage. That I stood tall with honor and dignity. However, I was so terrified of going on Space Mountain, that when we all read the sign warning us that if we had any heart condition we should not ride, I quickly pleaded, "I've got heartburn." Of course at the time I thought heartburn was a heart condition. I tried looking at my little brother in hopes he would save me by asking me to wait with him, but that request didn't come.

It was thirty minutes of horror. But, like all fears it was faced and I survived, yet none-the-less still afraid. It was great that I had faced my fears and lived to tell about it. But, unfortunately I still had about three E-tickets remaining. There was a part of me that wanted to lose these tickets "accidentally" thus avoiding having to go on any more roller coasters.

See back in the day when you went to Disneyland you paid for a book of tickets. When your ticket book was done you were done riding. Tickets went from A-E. You were given more of the A and B tickets and less of the others.

What I learned from that one day is that real joy and happiness do exist, and that we cannot have either without knowing real fear and pain and loss. I learned it is better to challenge your fears than to live in them; things are always better when you share them with those closest to you. Most of all, I learned that in life we only have but a few chances to take certain rides. Use them, don't lose them.

Oh, and I can't forget, *One day Leroy and I*…That story is for another time. Disneyland and I would live many more tales.

Courtyards

Apartments are strange in themselves. They all look the same—inside and out. They all have a courtyard and the same number of units. Our courtyard had a set of apartments facing each other that were identical—they were numbered 1-7—and I lived in lucky number seven. We lived upstairs and next to some Guedos— back when there were Guedos in the neighborhood. Around that time the barrio was still a "neighborhood". Not even half of it was Mexican.

I met my first friend in the courtyard behind the alley from mine. He was a Guedo named, Dwayne. On the other side of my courtyard was another Chinito named, Kenny. And, across the street from me was the only Negrito in the neighborhood, Leroy.

A courtyard has got to be one of the greatest things God ever invented. Our courtyard was everything from a park, to a soccer field, a boxing ring, and a kickball field, a picnic area, a reception hall, and not to forget a place to witness life at its best and worst. It was the hub of social life in the hood. Everything I needed to know I found out in my courtyard.

I learned to play hide-n-seek, freeze tag, Cowboys-n-Indians. I learned to kiss a girl in my courtyard. I learned that bees sting, and wasp sting twice as hard. I learned that Mexicans like to drink Budweiser and sing *corridos* at midnight. I made my best friends there.

I also learned that sap is sticky, and it hurts if you fall from a tree. I learned that I can't fly even if I put a towel around my neck and call it a cape—like Superman had. I learned that sometimes you gotta' stand up and fight for what you believe is right; and sometimes, *it's best to run away and live to fight another day.* I learned how to make a fort, and I learned that a window breaks when you throw a ball at it. I learned how to chase girls, and I learned that it hurts to get kicked in the *privates.*

Yup, I learned to stand, and I learned to fall. I learned to cry, and I learned to feel pain. I learned to be brave, and I learned to be afraid. I learned to have friends, and I learned to lose them. I learned to win and the thrill of it, and I learned to lose and the agony of it. I learned to laugh, and I learned to be teased. I learned to dust myself off, and I learned shame. I learned to tattletale, and I learned to take the blame.

Courtyards have rules. You don't just walk through anyone's courtyard and start running things and telling kids how to play tag, or kickball, or whatever game is being played. I'm *serious*...you'll get some rocks thrown your way. And, if you happen to be the kid who lives where the swimming pool is, or where the manager lives, you just have to find yourself a courtyard to belong to.

It is rare to have cross-courtyard mingling before the age of 10. Unless you create some sort of truce with the other courtyard it usually doesn't happen. And, if you ever get invited to play in another courtyard make sure you know who's in charge and you give the customary greeting: Hello, I'm just here visiting, feel free to abuse me and use me in any way you see fit, and excuse me now if I do anything to offend your way of life. This statement isn't actually said, but make sure it is implied in your eyes when you shake hands.

Jumping ahead, I'll never forget this one time when I was in the 3rd grade...poor David. Yup, David was a white boy. And, being the only white boy on the street, he lived the finer side of life when it came to toys. Well, David decided to play with us one day in Leroy's courtyard. He brought his toys—and they were nice, let me tell you. Well, Raymond, the kid in charge of our courtyard came out and decided he wanted to play too. Now, David didn't know anything about the customary greeting. So, when Raymond came over and took David's truck to play with it got a little ugly.

"Hey, that's *my* truck."

"So, I'm playing with it." Raymond gave David the opportunity to relinquish the truck without any incident. But, poor David, didn't know any better.

"No, it's *mine*." The next sound we heard was the thud of the truck against David's head. Immediately following that thud were David's cries for Momma.

"Take your truck." I guess Raymond was being nice that day; at least David got his truck back.

Dwayne

When we first moved into my barrio—I was just starting kindergarten—it was all a shock to me. I never had to really play with other kids before—I mean until my brother was born I grew up all alone on a ranch with my grandparents. My brother and I spent a lot of our time just playing with each other. We were real close. Probably because we weren't strangers to each other, and at the time I wasn't too fond of strangers.

I pretty much stayed to myself those first days of school. After about a week Dwayne, a kid in my class, started following me home—he reminded me of a dog I once had back on the ranch; it wasn't really my dog, but it followed me everywhere I went. Dwayne was annoying. He didn't stop talking for one second, which I guess was good because I wasn't saying much. He was a short kid, even for a five year old.

Anyway, one day his mother came over to my apartment and asked my mom if I could come over to their apartment and play with her son. Now this scared me a bit. I was heading into another man's courtyard—I didn't want to end up like David—and I didn't know the rules, and I was going to have to rely on Dwayne to lead the way.

In my short walk across two alleys I knew I was entering a new world. I had never been to Dwayne's courtyard before and already the atmosphere was changing as I strolled from my alley to his. The air was different. You see in my courtyard we were mostly Mexicans; so, we had Mexican smells. You always knew when it was time for supper because you could smell the fresh scent of tortillas, and beans being cooked on a daily basis. And when your throat got dry and your eyes started to burn you knew someone was cooking *chile*.

Once I got to his alley the aroma turned from Mexican food to some strange foreign scents—later I discovered those scents to be Vietnamese cooking, and some boiled cabbage that White folks love to eat. Then there it was...the gate. I was about to enter another realm. Where there were stories untold, and games unheard of, and adventures for the brave. And there it was at last, a brand new courtyard I had never seen before. I was in awe. There was a great palm in the center, and it was the longest courtyard I had ever seen. I couldn't see the end. It was so long it had a horizon...a horizon I tell you; and a sidewalk all around it—the sidewalks were the official big wheel racetracks. I wanted it. I wanted it all. My eyes had seen heaven and never wanted to leave.

There were so many kids playing so many games. There were kids skating, and riding, and hopping. I saw an inchworm, a pogo stick, a green machine, a Frisbee, a hoola-hoop; and kids playing hopscotch, and jump roping, and marbles...Oh, how I loved to play marbles...marbles of every color and size. There were big kids and little kids, AND PUPPIES. Wow, I had never seen puppies before. I get excited just talking about it. Yup, it was heaven I tell you.

Then...yup, then, I came up to his door. Before I could even ring the doorbell I could hear Dwayne running across the floor to the door—I have no idea how he always knew I was at his door before I rang.

"Hey, Isaac!" I never saw someone so excited to see me—even now.

"Come in...I got this new game...Mom, Isaac's here, can you get us some punch...You wanna see my cats...That's Larry over there—we named him after my uncle who looks just like him—and on top of the TV is Tigger—you know like on Winnie the Pooh. Doesn't he look just like him?" Dwayne always asked about thirty questions before you could answer the first one. I always ended up not answering any of them.

For a moment I wondered what "punch" was. It turns out it's Kool-aide—hey, you learn something new every day—but, I took some time to consider which was actually which. *Was Kool-aide the brand name for punch, or was punch the brand name for Kool-aide? Could Kool-aide be punch...could punch be Kool-aide? You know, kind of like how we call cotton swabs, Q-Tips?* Well, those were just the beginning of my youthful philosophies. All those questions Dwayne asked always gave me plenty of time to get lost in my thoughts.

Dwayne's house was full of stuff...just stuff. Stuff I had never seen before. One thing for sure he had a treasure in his kitchen. I saw so many boxes of every kind of cereal my eyes nearly popped right out. In my house we never had more than two boxes. And, we were never allowed to eat them without permission, and only for breakfast. I don't know why my mother guarded those cereal boxes so much—it was like they were made of gold.

Now it was time to run into his sister. I never had any sisters, and I'm sure glad of that now. Dwayne's sister was the poster child for not having one. Nothing in life had prepared me for this moment—there was this one time on the ranch when a coyote came scratching at my bedroom window and I got up to see what was there; I nearly stopped breathing I was so scared. She was a fiery redhead...like the devil I tell you. She had this shrieking voice like a cat when you step on its tail. I had never seen a redhead before, and I was sure she wasn't normal. And she had these spots all over her—it turns out they were just freckles. I'm telling you...you don't know fear until you look into the eyes of Satan himself and live to tell about it.

"*Mooom*, Dwayne's friend is staring at me." She belted.

For the next two hours it was Dwayne this, Dwayne that...Dwayne's friend this, and Dwayne's friend that. She was relentless with her annoyance. I did have a name you know. She never cared to use it; I was simply, Dwayne's friend.

Pong

Now when I was young playing inside the house was boring. There wasn't much in the house except parental supervision; and there always seemed to be more fun where mom wasn't around to watch...or hear. I mean outside there was a world of fun and adventure. Where there was a grass courtyard there were gymnastics, a wrestling ring, a boxing ring, a kickball field— basically an arena for every game known.

In my day we knew how to do cartwheels and round offs, climb a tree, and get dirty, catch bee's, and make weapons from pieces of wood we found—my favorite weapon was the nunchucks, which I usually made using an old window screen...ok, so sometimes I would just take the window screen off a vacant apartment.

But then came that day that changed not only my world but also the world of children everywhere. I had visited Dwayne's house early in the morning on the promise he had made that we would be playing a new game he had, and his mother would be serving *Kool-aide*, and cookies.

When I knocked on his door (oddly he wasn't at the door already) no one answered, but I could hear that awful sound of his sister's screechy voice.

"DWAYNE...YOUR LITTLE FRIEND IS HERE."

I heard nothing.

"DWAYNE...HE'S WAITING...ANSWER THE DOOR."

Again, I heard nothing.

"DWAYNE...DWAYNE...DWAYNE." Oh, God, would she just shut-up. I was begging for him to answer the door before my ears started to bleed.

Finally. "Hi Isaac...come in."

"Hey, Dwayne."

"Did you watch TV last night? Did you see the Incredible Hulk? (Remember when he turned Green...how about when he turned back to David Banner ... do you think I could be the Incredible Hulk? You want to play Incredible Hulk ... You can be Hulk and I'll be David Banner ... I got a bag just like his...you wanna see)" This line of questions went on forever it seemed, and it took some good training on my part to sift through it all and get to the point.

"Dwayne!!! Where's the game?" Not to be mean, but we would have gone through every question known to man before we started playing if I didn't interrupt.

"Come in my room."

Now, going into Dwayne's room wasn't a particularly fun thing for me. It meant two things. One, I was getting farther away from the front door. Two, Dwayne was obsessed with showing me everything in it, and the story behind it.

"Look, look..." He pointed to something, but I couldn't see anything that resembled any game I had ever seen. "Look, look..." He appeared to be pointing to the TV.

"I don't want to watch TV...I can do that at home." I said.

"No...it's on top of the TV." He cried in joy.

There it was. A little gray box with two controllers wired to it.

"What kind of fun are we going to have with your TV and a box? Am I supposed to throw this at you?" I thought.

I was confused to say the least; and not to mention completely disappointed in Dwayne's promise of a new game.

"Look…Look…" He turned the TV on. "Look…look…watch the screen."

He had the biggest smile and was panting like a dog in the sun. I was a little taken back by his excitement over what seemed to be nothing.

Then, all of a sudden my world changed. The bleep! Bleep! Bleep! Of the TV sound, and the image of a dot moving across the screen was like a hypnotic trance that left my mind blank. I couldn't remember my name…all I could think about was that bleep! Bleep! Bleep.

We must have played that game for over 2 hours (that seemed like a second). We played Pong Tennis, and Pong Handball. It was the greatest game ever. I had fallen in love for the first time. For the first time leaving Dwayne's house I felt sad. I felt a deep loss, like I was leaving a part of me behind. I was too young to know what love was, but I knew I couldn't live without Pong.

From that day forth Dwayne never had to beg me to come over. I ran over. I was there the second I got off the bus from school. I was there with a smile on my face and a warm spot in my heart for even his sister. I was all smiles.

Then that day came. I found out the truth that, *all good things come to an end.* It was as usual when I first arrived at Dwayne's house. Then it was all so different.

"Let's go outside and play…we can play marbles…or cars…or catch bees." Dwayne said excitedly.

"No Dwayne … let's play Pong."

"Well, we can't … my sister broke it last night."

"I did not."

"Yes you did … you jumped on me … and …"

I had known what it was to love something, to need something, to feel complete with it and live as though nothing else mattered. And, now, I was learning about loss, tragedy, and the wicked pain in your chest that stabs you as you feel love taken away.

"Wait…What happened?" I was shocked. "What happened to the Pong?"

"See Dwayne, your little friend doesn't want to be your friend anymore. He only liked you because he wanted to play Pong," she said.

"That's not true." He looked at me with those big eyes. "Hey Isaac, we can play my other games. I got all the board games. We can go outside and play marbles or we can catch bees."

A part of me wanted to be angry with Dwayne. A part of me just wanted to walk out the door and go home. But, looking into Dwayne's big puppy dog eyes, there was a part of me that felt something I had never felt before—shame. I was ashamed that I was using Dwayne's friendship. I was ashamed that I was his best friend, but he wasn't mine. I was ashamed that I wanted to go home.

I also felt something else I never felt before—Friendship. Dwayne was a good friend. Why? Because all he wanted from me was me. He wanted me to be there. Whether it was to play Pong, or to play nothing, he wanted to be with me.

I couldn't take the look in Dwayne's eyes anymore. I had to make a choice right then and there: to be or not to be Dwayne's friend.

"Come on Dwayne…let's play outside…I'm tired of being inside all day anyway."

PEGGY P. EDWARDS

GLORIA ALLRED Y YO

La famosa (infame para algunos) licenciada Gloria Allred estuvo casi a punto de representarme una vez, hace tiempo. En 1990 ya bien se conocía la abogada por representar a mujeres abusadas por hombres famosos.

En aquel tiempo yo era la Directora de la Fundación de Inmigrantes de América (FIA), una organización no lucrativa dedicada a ayudar a los inmigrantes. Les ayudábamos en hacerse residentes y ciudadanos; les ayudábamos hacerse parte de la comunidad norteamericana. A causa del gran servicio que ofrecíamos, crecimos enormemente en esos dos años. Amnistía, que se pasó por la administración de Reagan en 1986, sacó a millones de indocumentados de la sombra. Una vez documentados, reunieran a sus familias que se reunieran con ellos. Calificamos para medio millón de dólares del gobierno para pagar a maestros que les enseñaban inglés, abogados, que los representaban, y pagaba la renta de un local dentro de la iglesia Metodista en la avenida Santa Ana, California.

Parecía que todo caminaba de maravilla, hasta que mi secretaria me señaló que personajes extraños, vestidos en camuflaje que usaban botas militares, aparecían a menudo y siempre camino a la oficina del que era nuestro abogado.

Yo le había ofrecido un puesto en nuestra mesa directiva a este supuesto abogado. Algo me decía que no era derecho, pero ignoré mi intuición y él aceptó mi invitación, y luego pidió oficina. No pasó mucho tiempo antes de que manipulara para hacerse Director de la mesa directiva. Interrumpía las reuniones y se hacía cargo. A mí me hizo a un lado. Al principio no lo tomé muy en serio, *después de todo*, pensé, *estamos en el mismo equipo*. (Pero el nunca mencionó a los intrusos de camuflaje).

Luego pasó lo inimaginable -- un día llegué al trabajo sólo para encontrar a gente que marchaba alrededor de nuestro edificio, cargando carteles diciendo que yo era racista. Estaba asombrada. No me podía imaginar de dónde esto venía. Yo había llegado al extremo de sacar un préstamo sobre mi hipoteca. Soy de México y totalmente bilingüe. Trabajé por años ayudando a los inmigrantes; siempre fueron mi primera consideración. Peleé duro por la Amnistía. Fui a la capital, Washington D.C., para abogar en su favor. ¿Cómo era posible que alguien pensara que yo era racista?

El siguiente paso del abogado fue tratar de sacarme de mi propia Fundación. Se pasaba el tiempo tratando de enajenar a mis amigos y mi apoyo. Se reunía en secreto en su oficina tras llave. Me comenzaron a llegar llamadas amenazadoras, y tiraban piedras a mi parabrisas cuando llegaba al trabajo.

Lo más grave ocurrió cuando el gobierno depositó medio millón de dólares en nuestra cuenta bancaria. El licenciado y sus sicarios corrieron al banco tan pronto supieron la noticia y atentaron sacar los fondos. El gobierno sospechó una mala jugada y congeló nuestros fondos. Ahora no podíamos pagar a nuestros empleados, ni la renta del edificio.

Tristemente las cosas empeoraban. Camino a casa un atardecer, mi carro se detuvo en la autopista 5. Esperé largo rato pero nadie paró para ayudarme. Finalmente me salí del coche para conseguir ayuda. Desafortunadamente me torcí el tobillo, quedé coja y me quedé en casa los próximos dos días.

Cuando regresé a mi oficina estaba cerrada con llave con un cerrojo nuevo. Un letrero en mi puerta decía, *"¡Lárgate, ya no se te necesita aquí!"* Se me rompió el corazón, que podía hacer? Pero también tenía miedo, tenía que encontrar ayuda de inmediato.

Le hablé a la Licenciada Gloria Allred. La había visto en las noticias. Su secretaria escuchó mi caso, y no tardó en hablarme para informarme que la famosa Gloria Allred escucharía mi caso. Esto me dio esperanza de que no todo estuviera perdido.

Aparecí en su oficina el día acordado. Vestía mi elegante traje *St.John's Knit* que me quedaba como guante. Pero estaba preocupada, distraída, desenfocada. La cita con la Lic. Gloria Allred era lo único bueno que me había ocurrido parecía, en mucho tiempo.

Gloria salió de su despacho, me miró de arriba para abajo con una mirada de desprecio, se dio la media vuelta y regresó a su despacho, cerrando la puerta. Su secretaria entonces igual me miró y dijo, "La licenciada Gloria Allred no se encargará de su caso, adiós y buena suerte."

Mi esperanza despedazada, lagrimas mojándome las mejillas, regresé a mi carro. Cabizbaja, de pronto me miré – y me di cuenta. Vestía mi elegante traje *St John's Knit*, que me quedaba como guante, al revés, costuras y etiquetas afuera, a la vista. ¡Qué trágico, pero sin poderme parar, me puse a reír!

Después de eso dejé mi querida FIA. Pensaba que la gente, que tanto había ayudado, no querrían verme muerta – el abigaducho y sus monigotes harían cualquier cosa por dinero y poder. El gobierno no tardó en cerrar la Fundación.

Pero la vida es un pañuelito. Yo ahora vivo en un pueblo de retirados en el sur de California – es un verdadero paraíso. Se mantiene tan bello por nuestros jardineros. Un día platicando con uno de ellos nos reconocimos. Él me dijo que nosotros le habíamos ayudado a documentarse, aprender inglés, integrarse a la comunidad e inmigrar a su familia. Dijo que había ayudado a más personas que me imaginaba; dijo que un lugar muy especial me aguardaba en el cielo. Yo doy gracias que por lo menos pude ayudar a algunos.

GLORIA ALLRED AND ME

The famous (infamous to some) attorney Gloria Allred almost agreed to represent me once upon a time. Back in 1990 she already had a reputation for representing women victims of famous men.

I was, at the time CEO of American Immigrant Foundation (AIF), a 501c3 nonprofit dedicated to assisting immigrants. We helped them become residents and citizens; we helped them become part of the American community. Because of the great service we offered, we grew exponentially in a short couple of years. Amnesty, passed by the Reagan administration in 1986, had brought millions out of the shadows. Once they became documented, they petitioned for relatives to join them. We qualified for a half million in SLIAG government funds to pay for teachers who taught them English, attorneys, who represented them, and the rental of a Methodist church building on Santa Ana Boulevard in Santa Ana, California.

It seemed all was going better than well, until my secretary pointed out that strange characters, dressed in camouflage and wearing army boots, were appearing quite often, and always on their way to our, at the time, attorney's office.

I had offered this lawyer a position on our Board of Directors. Something told me he was not quite right, but I ignored my intuition and he accepted the position, he then asked for an office. It wasn't long before he had contrived to become our BOD President. He disrupted meetings and took over. I was pushed aside. At first I didn't take it too seriously, *after all,* I thought, *we're on the same team.* (But he never mentioned the camouflaged intruders).

Much to my surprise, I arrived at work one day to find people marching around our building carrying posters claiming that I was a racist. I was truly shocked. I couldn't imagine where this came from. I had gone so far as to take a loan out on the equity of our home. I am from Mexico and totally bilingual. I had spent years helping immigrants; they had always been my first consideration. I had fought hard for Amnesty. I had lobbied our politicians and had even travelled to Washington D.C. How could anyone possibly think I could be a racist?

The lawyer's next move was to try to remove me from my own Foundation. He spent his time trying to alienate my friends and support. He held secret meetings in his office behind a locked door. I started getting threatening phone calls and rocks were thrown at my windshield when I arrived at work.

The epitome of his wickedness occurred when the government deposited half a million dollars in our AIF account. The lawyer and his minions rushed to the bank as soon as they heard the news and attempted to draw out the funds. The government suspected foul play and froze our SLIAG funds. Now we couldn't pay employee salaries or the rental of the church building.

Sadly things were becoming even worse. On the way home one late evening, my car stalled on the 5 Freeway. I waited quite a while but nobody stopped to help. Finally I got out of my car to flag someone down. Unfortunately I twisted my ankle; was crippled, and stayed home for the next couple of days.

When I returned to my office it had a new lock that was locked. There was a sign on my door saying I no longer worked there. It said, "Get out of town, you are no longer welcome here." I was heartbroken, what could I do? But I was also scared. I needed help soon.

I called Atty. Gloria Allred; I had seen her on the news. Her secretary listened to my story and it wasn't long before I got a call saying Gloria Allred herself would listen to my case. This gave me hope that all was not lost.

I appeared at her office on that scheduled date. I was wearing my red knit St. John suit that fit me like a glove. But still, I was worried, I was devastated, I was stressed. An appointment with Gloria Allred was all the good news I had heard in what seemed a very long time.

Gloria came out of her office and looked me up and down. There was a sneer of disappointment drawn across her face. She walked out of the waiting room, back to her office and closed the door, without uttering one single word. Her secretary approached, and with a look of disgust said, "Atty. Gloria Allred will not take your case. Good luck and goodbye."

My hopes dashed, tears running down my cheeks, I returned to my car. I hung my head in dejection then noticed...I was wearing my red knit St. John suit, that fit me like a glove, inside out – the tags and the seams were all sticking out. Yes, it was tragic, but I started to laugh.

After that I quit AIF. I knew that the people I helped in so many ways didn't want me dead. The nefarious lawyer and his gang would do anything for money and power. The government shut down the AIF nonprofit and it soon disappeared.

But life has many paths, twists and turns and you can't be sure just where they will lead. I now live in a retirement village in southern California – a real paradise. It is kept lovely by our gardeners. One day, chatting with one of them we recognized each other. He said we had helped him get documented, learn English, become part of the community, and immigrate his family. He said I had helped more people than I knew; he said there was a special place in heaven for me. I am thankful I could at least help some.

CHARLES REDNER

VISTA DESDE MI CELDA MEXICANA

Mientras escribía una novela enfocada en el narcoterrorismo en ambos lados de la frontera, decidí viajar el rumbo que se tomaría...

Salimos de Tucson en nuestra camioneta al amanecer – seis turistas – además de dos norteamericanos hispario parlantes, nuestro guía norteamericano, y yo, el autor. La camioneta llega a Nogales, Arizona, una hora más tarde donde lo único necesario para cruzar la frontera a México, es una gran sonrisa. Veinte minutos más tarde, en el retén militar, se nos requiere una visa de turista. La espera por la visa va de despacio a más despacio.

Esperamos.

Entonces nuestro guía nos aconseja. Parece que el departamento de visas está muy ocupado hoy, aunque sólo vemos tres otros solicitantes en la oficina. Pero, si pudiéramos dar una propina (no mordida), quizás se pueda apurar el tramite – quizás $10 por persona. Ponemos $80 en el mostrador y rápidamente estamos volando por la carretera 15, rumbo a Hermosillo, 225 kilómetros de la frontera.

Continuamos otros setenta-y-cinco kilómetros y pasamos la noche en el precioso Golfo de California, en el pueblo de San Carlos. Nuestro casi-lujoso hotel mira sobre el puerto y se parece al lujo de Newport Beach de California, aunque no con tantos yates.

Después del desayuno la próxima mañana, pasamos por Ciudad Obregón y seguimos a Navajoa, donde damos vuelta al este hacía nuestro destino, Álamos. Algunos dicen que este pueblo colonial situado en las montañas recuerda a San Miguel Allende de otros tiempos. Nos alojamos en una residencia que en el pasado fue convento de monjas. Cada uno es llevado a una celda.

Se siente encantador. Me siento en mi cama e inspecciono un cuarto inmaculadamente limpio de tres por cuatro metros cuadrados. No hay mucho lugar considerando los muebles y la puerta que da al baño. De pronto me doy cuenta de mi aislamiento y me siento cómodo – sin radio, televisión, teléfono, red, y empleados que no hablan inglés.

Ahora mi corazón late más despacio, más a lo mexicano. Mi cuerpo entero me parece extranjero pues de pronto camina tan lento. Me siento a gusto y cómodo en mi nuevo ajuste de ambiente.

Los siguientes días, mientras el guía guiaba a sus encargados, yo me quedaba haciendo lo mío, explorando como yo quería. Después de todo, esta no era una vacación. Yo, se suponía, estaba encontrándome con una pandilla de terroristas que tomarían su parte en las páginas de mi futuro libro.

Mientras aprendí cosas importantes, por ejemplo, hay más que una plaza en Álamos. Hay una en frente para los turistas y otra por la callejuela donde compran los poblanos. Me senté con los del pueblo e investigué. Fui a la estación de camiones algo descuidada. Tomé fotos del mercado abierto para mi futura referencia.

Platiqué con los niños, es asombroso lo que puedes aprender de un lugar si le pides a los papás que te permitan platicar con sus hijos – ellos a menudo hablan más abiertamente sobre un lugar.

La oportunidad de agregar el color local a mi historia viene viernes, cuando soy testigo de algo que sólo conocía en los cuentos de mi amigo de Cádiz, España – el cortejo – Paso a Rosa.

Los adolescentes se sientan alrededor de la plaza mientras las jóvenes caminan. De vez en cuando un adolescente se levanta y le regala una rosa a una joven. Ella la acepta y sigue su camino. Cuando lo pasa por segunda vez, o se queda con la rosa y él ahora la acompaña, o se la regresa tristemente, su invitación rechazada (pero ahora la rosa es de nuevo disponible para otra bonita señorita).

La semana terminó demasiado rápido. Yo aun no estaba listo para regresar al norte, "a tiempos normales en los Estados Unidos," pero nuestro chofer y sus pasajeros tenían que volver. Este viaje fue único entre varios al D.F., Monterrey, Taxco y otros.

No alojarnos en los conocidos hoteles, Hilton, Omni, y Ritz-Carlton en esta ocasión, quedándonos en lugares locales, me hizo poner atención especial al tiempo y al lugar. Me dio un recuerdo inolvidable que en mis cuentos recuerdo con cariño. No escribí ni mi nombre ni la fecha en la pared de mi celda, aunque tuve la tentación. Quería que otros que se quedaran en el mismo lugar supieran que yo allí, en mi celda mexicana, pasé un tiempo maravilloso.

VIEW FROM MY MEXICAN CELL

Before finishing a novel engaging terrorist travelling through Mexico to cause mayhem in the United States, I explored a route that they might travel.

We depart Tucson in a van at dawn—six tourists plus two Spanish-speaking, Norte Americano driver-guides and me, the writer. The van reaches Nogales, Arizona an hour later, where a big smile is all that's needed to cross into Mexico. Twenty minutes later at the military checkpoint, we are required to obtain a visitor's visa. The work pace behind the counter progresses from slow, to slow, to Mexican slow.

We wait.

Our guide huddles with us. It seems that the visa department is extremely busy today, although we only see three other applicants waiting in the room. However, if we could see our way to offer a tip (let's not say bribe), the service might be expedited—perhaps $10 US each. This is an all-or-nothing offer. We plop $80 US on the counter and quickly thereafter are zooming down Highway 15 south to Hermosillo some 225 km below the border.

We continue another seventy-five kilometers and spend the night in the gorgeous *Golfo de California* town of San Carlos. Our near-luxury hotel overlooks the harbor and is reminiscent of the wealth found in Newport Beach, albeit with a few less yacht slips.

After breakfast the next morning, we drive through Ciudad Obregon then onto Navojoa, where we turn east toward our final destination, Alamos. Some say that this colonial, mountain town reminds them of San Miguel Allende of years earlier. We are to be quartered in a residence once built to house cloistered nuns. Each of us is shown to a cell.

It feels enchanting. I sit on my hard bunk and survey the immaculately clean 9 x12 foot space. Not much room to move around, given the furnishing and doorway access to the one-person-wide bathroom. Sudden awareness of my isolation becomes a comfort—no radio, no television, no phone (cell or otherwise), no Internet, and the staff does not speak English.

At this point my heart rate slowed to Mexican slow. My entire being downshifted to a gear that I didn't know I possessed.

Within hours, I had acclimated to my surroundings. It felt more than comfortable.

For the next few days, while the guide took his charges to see the sights, I became the outsider, choosing to travel my own way. After all, I was not on holiday; I was reconnoitering for a fictitious group of terrorists who would be passing through on the pages of my novel.

There is more than one plaza in Alamos. There is one in front of the church for the tourists, and one through an alleyway where the locals shop. I sat among the residents and scouted. I hung around the grubby-looking bus station. I took pictures of the open markets for future reference. I talked with the children. It's amazing how much you can learn about a place by asking parents if you may speak with their children—usually they have less resistance to telling the truth about a place.

The opportunity to add local color to my story comes on a Friday night, when I witness something that I had only heard about from my friend born in Cadiz, Spain—a different kind of courtship—*Paso a Rosa.*

Teenage boys sit on benches around the plaza and the young women walk continually around. As the ladies pass, a boy will jump up and hand a rose to one. She accepts it and continues walking. When she passes him the second time, she either keeps the rose and the boy joins her on the walk, or sadly, she may give it back and his invitation has been rejected (but the rose is once again available for the next pretty señorita).

The week ended all too soon. I was not ready to speed back up to "U.S. Normal Time," but my ride and escort needed to return his passengers. On this trip, I experienced Mexico like none of my previous visits to Mexico City, Monterey, Taxco or the border towns.

Avoiding the Hilton, Omni, and Ritz-Carlton for once, I went native, as it were, and paid very special attention to the element of time. It was a writing/research retreat I'll always remember fondly. I managed to refrain from carving my name and date on the wall of my cell, although the urge was surely there. I wanted others who stay after me to know that I spent a delightful time in this Mexican cell.

ROBERT M. GLEAVES

NERUDA & LORCA: A MEETING OF POETIC MINDS

*Si pudiera llorar de miedo en una casa sola, si pudiera sacarme los ojos y comermelos, lo haria por tu voz de naranjo enlutado y port tu poesia que sale dando gritos. (*Pablo Neruda, "Oda a Federico García Lorca"*).*

On October 13, 1933, Federico García Lorca arrived in Buenos Aires, Argentina, to attend the American debut of his play *Bodas de sangre (Blood Wedding)* and to lecture to literary groups in the area. On that day he was introduced to the Chilean poet Pablo Neruda, who was then serving as Chilean consul to Argentina. As Emir Rodríguez Monegal observes, "The date is marked with a white stone in Hispanic poetry of this century... They (Lorca and Neruda) form a friendship which only death will correct, and they establish a lasting bridge between the two shores of new Spanish-language poetry."[1]

This meeting brought together two major lyricists from different parts of the Spanish-speaking world, and literary critics have not yet measured the cross-cultural impact of this Lorca-Neruda friendship. Neruda himself, however, expressed indebtedness to Lorca in the elaboration of his poetic style. Especially striking today is the admiration that the two poets so eloquently expressed for each other. For example, on December 6, 1934, Lorca introduced Neruda to a lecture group as "one of those authentic poets who have their senses attuned to a world which is not ours and which few persons can perceive. A poet closer to death than to philosophy, closer to sentiment with its attendant pain than to intellect, closer to blood than to ink. A poet filled with mysterious voices, which fortunately he himself is unable to decipher... Pablo Neruda's poetry rises up with a tone of passion, tenderness and sincerity never before equaled in America."[2]

Lorca's praise of Neruda is matched only by Neruda's eloquent writings and public speeches on Federico, especially those presented after the latter's death in 1936. It was in Paris that Neruda gave an emotional lecture on Lorca in 1937, for example. South of the Pyrenees the Spanish Civil War was raging, and the memory of Lorca was fresh in the minds of this group gathered in the French capital to pay tribute to the fallen poet: Federico García Lorca! He was down to earth like a folk guitar, cheerful, melancholic, profound and yet transparent like a child, like the common people. If they had launched a careful search into every corner of Spain for someone to offer in sacrifice, as one sacrifices a symbol, they could not have found anyone better than Lorca to represent the popular soul of Spain, in quickness and in depth. Those who wanted to fire their bullets into the heart of their Race selected well on gunning him down."[3]

In the above statement, Neruda praises Lorca as a person and national symbol, without making direct reference to his talents as a poet. Even today, critics and former acquaintances of Lorca find it difficult to discuss his literary production apart from his personality and tragic involvement with the Spanish Civil War. Lorca was a charismatic figure, admired for his talents as a poet, dramatist, musician, and painter, but popular especially because he radiated charm and gaiety wherever he appeared, and Neruda was obviously attracted to this aspect of his Spanish friend's personality: "He was the most loved, the most cherished, of all Spanish poets, and he was the closest to being a child, because of his marvelous happy temperament."[4] In a passage from Neruda's memoirs which provides a reliable synthesis of his attitude towards Lorca, he emphasizes Federico's cheerful, engaging personality:

What a poet! I have never seen grace and genius, a winged heart and a crystalline waterfall, come together in anyone else as they did in him. Federico García Lorca was the extravagant "duende", his was a magnetic joyfulness that generated a zest for life in his heart and radiated it like a planet. Openhearted and comical, worldly and provincial, an extraordinary musical talent, a splendid mime, easily alarmed and superstitious, radiant and noble, he was the epitome of Spain through the ages, of her popular tradition. Of Arabic-Andalusian roots, he brightened and perfumed like jasmine the stage set of a Spain that, alas, is gone forever (*Memoirs,* p. 122*).*

It must not be assumed, however, that Lorca exuded optimism at every moment. There was a dark side to his personality, and much of his poetry clearly illustrates his righteous indignation at social injustice and at the violence perpetrated in the name of authority or material progress, and especially his curious attraction to and fear of death, which is a constant theme in his poetry. He was so acutely sensitive to the subject that he almost seemed clairvoyant in interpreting several events as prophetic of his tragic death. Neruda, for example, mentions that Lorca sensed his approaching execution on witnessing a scene in which some wild pigs attacked and killed a gentle lamb, which was accompanying him on a solitary walk in a small Castilian town. Federico, still shaken from the memory of this bloody scene, told the story to Pablo three months before the outbreak of the Civil War, and the Chilean poet reacted thus: "Later on I saw, more and more clearly, that the incident had been a vision of his own death, the premonition of his incredible tragedy (*Memoirs*, p. 124).

Lorca's death had a profound effect on Neruda's poetry, as we shall see later. The initial mystery is that two poets of such dissimilar backgrounds should meet and discover that their attitudes toward poetry and life were so similar. It is these similarities that assume primary importance in determining the significance of that meeting in Buenos Aires in 1933.

Even the casual reader will find major differences between Lorca and Neruda on reading their poetry, and it would serve no useful purpose to attempt to minimize those differences. However, it is precisely in one difference — their choice of atmospheric background — that we find an important similarity in their approach to lyric poetry. Undeniably, Lorca and Neruda are universal poets, but they bring to their poetry the geographical and cultural setting of their formative years. It would be difficult, for example, to understand most of Lorca's works without some familiarity with the Andalusian motifs of the gypsy, the *cante jondo,* the bullfight with its cult of death, the visualization of such typical scenes as a brilliant sun striking the tile roofs of whitewashed houses in hillside villages, calling to mind the southern Spanish love for brilliant colors. In a more subtle way, one must also be familiar with the air of antiquity that permeates the area, for the roots of Andalusia go deep. Allen Josephs and Juan Caballero, in an excellent introduction to Lorca's poetry, state categorically that "all of Lorca's work is unmistakably Andalusian and even indecipherable without this Andalusian presence,"[5] and they are careful to distinguish between the Andalusia of the tourist poster and that *Andalucía milenaria* so important in Lorca's works.

Neruda, like Lorca, was almost umbilically attached to his native land, despite the fact that he traveled widely throughout his life and was able to reside in other countries for long periods before returning to Chile for sustenance. Although his poetry does not have an exclusively Chilean ambience to the same degree that most of Lorca's poems have an Andalusian ambience, it is evident that the rainy, cold atmosphere of Neruda's native province left a clear imprint on his works, especially in the gray or colorless settings often present in his poems. If Lorca's poetry is acted out on a brightly lit stage, reminding us of Spain's sunny southland, many of Neruda's poems appear to take place indoors on a dull, wintry day or night. He begins his memoirs with the following words: "I'll start out by saying this about the days and the years of my childhood: the rain was the one unforgettable presence for me then. The great southern rain, coming down like a waterfall from the Pole, from the skies of Cape Horn to the frontier. On this frontier, my country's Wild West, I first opened my eyes to life, the land, poetry, and the rain" (*Memoirs,* p. 6).

Perhaps the clearest evidence of Neruda's affection for Chile and indebtedness to his native land can be found in one of his speeches, made in 1962, in which he states that "my biggest and longest book has been this book which we call Chile. I have never ceased reading my fatherland; I have never taken my eyes from that long stretch of territory." He continues thus:

In my travels through the Far East I comprehended very little of what I experienced. Furthermore, I could not relate to the dry hills of that mysterious and metallic Peru, or to the vastness of the Argentine pampas. However much I loved Mexico, perhaps I was never capable of understanding that country either... Here in Chile my experience has always been different. My heart — through which so much time has passed — is still moved by those wooden houses, those shabby streets which begin at Victoria and end in Puerto Montt, and which make musical sounds like a guitar as the wind blows through... I am a poet-patriot, a nationalist molded with the clay of Chile. Our passionate, soul-stirring homeland.[6]

Chile, therefore, not only served as a spiritual anchor for Neruda's soul: it was also the only country that he truly understood emotionally and intellectually.

Roy Campbell once referred to Andalusia as Lorca's *querencia,* and perhaps the same could be said of central Chile for Neruda. Campbell's observations regarding the *querencia* are illuminating, and apply almost equally to the two poets:

Andalusia is Lorca's querencia. The querencia is the exact spot that every Spanish fighting bull chooses to return to, between his charges, in the arena. It is his invisible fortress or camp.

During Lorca's sojourns abroad, or in Madrid, he always returned for poetical strength to his native province; even when he did not return to it in person, he returned in imagination, memory, and dreams: and it never failed him as a source of strength and inspiration.[7]

It should be emphasized that Lorca and Neruda, despite close ties with their native countries, were not excessively nationalistic. In an interview published in 1936, Lorca admits, "It would be impossible for me to live outside my geographical limits," but he reveals immediately his attitudes toward nationalistic chauvinism:

I am a full-blooded Spaniard, and it would be impossible for me to leave outside my geographic limits, but I detest the person who is Spanish simply for the sake of being Spanish. I am a brother to all people, and I denounce the man who sacrifices himself for an abstract nationalistic idea for the sole reason that he has a blind love for his homeland. The good Chinese is closer to me than the bad Spaniard. I sing to Spain and I feel her to my marrow; but first of all I am a universal man and everyone's brother. Naturally, I do not believe in political frontiers. (*LOC,* p. 1817)

Neruda, like Lorca, expresses disdain towards those persons who attempt to label him a Chilean as opposed to a member of the human race:

Me han hablado de Venezuelas,
de Paraguayes y de Chiles,
no sé de lo que están hablando:
conozco la piel de la tierra
y sé que no tiene apellido.

They have spoken to me of Venezuelas,
Of Chiles and of Paraguays;
I have no idea of what they are saying.
I know only the skin of the earth
And I know it is without a name.
("Demasiadoes nombres," *NOC,* II, p. 681; trans. Alastair Reed)

This affirmation of the brotherhood of man leads us to a consideration of the general political attitudes of Lorca and Neruda during the period that they were friends. From our perspective today, we could argue that Lorca was essentially apolitical, while Neruda was an outspoken member of the Communist Party and a close friend of Chile's Marxist president, Salvador Allende (1970-73). At the time of their meeting in Buenos Aires, however, both authors were above all literary figures, and not political activists. With the approach of the Spanish Civil War both supported the Republican cause, but Lorca chose to refrain from participation in the political process, while Neruda was prevented from involvement because of his diplomatic status in Spain as Chilean consul. Prior to 1936 neither author used his poetry as a vehicle for political propaganda. Clearly, both were drawn into the political arena by the sheer force of the Spanish Civil War, as we shall see later.

In 1927, Neruda was sent on his first diplomatic mission to the Orient, where he was to dedicate four years to consular duties in Burma, Ceylon, India, Java, and China. In May of 1929 Lorca departed for the United States, where he spent most of the following year in New York City, returning to Spain via Cuba in the summer of 1930. The two poets were not acquainted with each other during that period, but these trips abroad appear to have acted upon them in similar ways, leading both in new directions toward a poetry of alienation and existential anguish, stimulated in part by their encounters with people and political systems foreign to their understanding and sense of values. Lorca's evocation of Wall Street as a symbol of New York City illustrates just how much he suffered from culture shock:

One is impressed with its coldness and cruelty. Gold arrives in rivers from all parts of the earth, and death arrives with it. In no other part of the world does one feel such a total absence of human spirit… Frightening scenes of suicides, of people suffering from hysteria or fainting in large groups. Terrible scenes, but without grandeur.

Horrible. Nobody can imagine the solitude that a Spaniard — especially a man from the South — feels in that place. (*LOC*, p. 1715)

Neruda, too, was overwhelmed by his first experiences abroad, and, while denying that Oriental philosophy influenced him in the composition of *Residencia en la Tierra (Residence on Earth),* he freely admits that the political climate, social conditions, and his own feelings of solitude were major factors in determining the type of verse that he was producing at that time:

In the India of those years there was little room for deep contemplation for one's navel. An existence that made brutal physical demands, a colonial position based on the most cold-blooded degradation, thousands dying every day of cholera, smallpox, fever, and hunger, a feudal society thrown into chaos by India's immense population and industrial poverty, stamped such great ferocity on life that all semblance of mysticism disappeared.

I don't believe, then, that my poetry during this period reflected anything but the loneliness of an outsider transplanted to a violent, alien world. (*Memoirs,* p. 84)

It is largely because Neruda and Lorca both suffered from this "loneliness of an outsider transplanted to a violent, alien world" that *Poeta en Nueva York (Poet in New York),* written in 1929 and 1930, and *Residencia de la Tierra,* composed between 1925 and 1935, are really quite similar to each other in tone and theme. The two authors, although denying any affiliation with French Surrealism, begin to express their existential anguish through the cultivation of elegantly surrealistic images, almost devoid of logical correspondences, as a reflection of the nightmarish chaos of the worlds they are attempting to portray. The comparison of resemblances between these two books deserves detailed study, but we can state that *Poeta en Nueva York* and *Residencia de la Tierra,* through the projection of obscure and often surrealistic imagery, present a pessimistic view of a world in which death is the only reason for living. These two books signal a political awakening for both poets, though commitment to a specific political cause is not yet in evidence.

By 1933, Neruda and Lorca had just passed through similar phases in their lives and in the elaboration of their poetry. Therefore, it is not surprising that they considered themselves kindred spirits from the moment of their meeting. Their common dedication to the poetic art in general also helped to draw them together. Shortly after Lorca's arrival in Argentina, the two poets presented a lecture *al alimón* in tribute to Rubén Darío, in which they alternated in the reading of a prepared text on the Nicaraguan poet, as in the following:

NERUDA: Ladies...

LORCA: ...and gentlemen: In bullfighting there is what is known as "bullfighting *al alimon,* in which two toreros, holding one cape between them, outwit the bull together.

NERUDA: Linked as if by an electrical impulse, Federico and I will together thank you for this prestigious reception.[9]

This public meeting of poetic minds is symbolic of the personal harmony and common attitudes toward poetry that prevailed between Lorca and Neruda throughout the two years and ten months that the two were in contact with each other. From the time of Neruda's arrival in Spain on a diplomatic mission in 1934, the two men spent many hours together and made numerous joint appearances for lectures and poetry recitals.

Neruda's fame as a lyricist was enhanced by his contacts with the Spanish poets in Madrid at that time, for Lorca was able to open doors for him in Spanish intellectual circles. Vicente Aleixandre, Rafael Alberti, and Miguel Hernández established close relationships with Neruda as a result of his sojourn in Spain, while the older poet Juan Ramón Jiménez was irritated by the prestige that the Chilean writer was enjoying in Madrid. Juan Ramón's vicious attacks on the younger poet stem primarily from Neruda's advocacy of a *poesía sin pureza,* as outlined in an essay published in the first issue of his journal *Caballo Verde para la Poesia (A Green Horse for Poetry),* which appeared in Madrid in 1935.

For Neruda, any topic is fair game for the lyric poet in search of inspiration. Furthermore, Neruda affirms in his memoirs that "a poet can write for a university or a labor union, for skilled workers and professionals" (*Memoirs,* p. 267). Such attitudes are in direct opposition to Jiménez's view of poetry as a pure art form — *poesía desnuda,* as he called it — and he obviously was personally offended by the attention that Neruda received for his attacks on pure poetry. García Lorca concurred with Neruda in rejecting the concept of "naked poetry," though we cannot be certain whether his comments in *El Sol* in 1936 were made in context of the Neruda-Jiménez polemic: "This concept of art for art's sake would be cruel if it were not so ridiculous. No true man still believes in that nonsense about *arte puro.* In this dramatic moment in the world the artist should cry and laugh with his people. We must leave aside the bouquet of lilies and step in the mud up to our waists to assist those who are searching for the lilies." (*LOC,* p. 1814)

Today one cannot judge precisely Neruda's impact on Lorca as a person or poet, even though the personal affinity is obvious and Neruda emphasizes in his writings the admiration that he and Federico felt for each other's poetry: "García Lorca's monumental command of metaphor seduced me, and everything he wrote attracted me. For his part, he would sometimes ask me to read him my latest poems, and halfway through the reading he would break in, shouting, "Stop, stop, I'm letting myself be influenced by you!" (*Memoirs,* p. 122). Nonetheless, one should be wary of assigning "influences" of one author on another. Indeed, it has been my intention only to indicate some points of contact between Lorca and Neruda in their personal lives and some clear similarities between the two in their attitudes toward poetry. It is appropriate, however, after the points of contact between the two have been established, to acknowledge the enormous impact that Lorca's death and the ensuing Spanish Civil War had on the direction of Neruda's poetry.

It would be naïve to assert that Lorca "invented Neruda," as Pedro Henríquez Ureña suggested in a conversation with Jorge Guillén: "Yes, he departed Spain much more famous than when he arrived in Madrid."[10] On the other hand, the senseless execution of Federico in Viznar is a documentable factor in directing Neruda's poetry away from general existential anguish toward specific preoccupation with political and social themes, and toward the use of more straightforward language than we can find in *Residencia de la Tierra,* though perhaps no more straightforward than the language of his early love poems.

Neruda's anger and deep sadness over Lorca's death are treated in the text of his Paris speech of 1937 and in such writings as *Viajes (Travels),* in his memoirs, entitled *Confieso que he vivido (I Confess That I Have Lived),* and in his moving apocalyptic poem, "Explico algunas cosas" (I'm Explaining a Few Things"), from *Tercera Residencia (Third Residence),* published in 1947, not to be confused with the first two *Residencias,* written before Lorca's death. In this poem Neruda explains the changes that took place within him as a result of the Civil War, and how these changes led naturally to a shift in the subject matter and tone of his poetry; then he evokes the horrors of the Spanish war, concluding with the following lines:

Preguntaréis por qué su poesía
No nos habla del sueño, de las hojas,
De los grandes volcanes de su pais natal?
Venid a ver la sangre por las calles.
Venid a ver
La sangre por las calles,
Venid a ver la sangre
Por las calles!

And you will ask: why doesn't his poetry
Speak of dreams and leaves
And the great volcanoes of his native land?
Come and see the blood in the streets,
Come and see
The blood in the streets.
Come and see the blood
In the streets!
(*NOC*, 1, p. 272-3; trans. Nathaniel Tarn)

The above poem mentions Lorca briefly ("Federico, do you remember/from under the ground/where the light of June drowned flowers in your mouth?"), but Neruda is pointing primarily toward the Civil War in general as a factor in guiding him toward a poetry of political commitment. The following passage by the Chilean poet provides the key to understanding the emotional impact of Federico García Lorca's dead on the life and literary career of Pablo Neruda:

> For me, it started on the evening of July 19, 1936. A resourceful and pleasant Chilean, Bobby Deglané, was a wrestling promoter in Madrid's huge Circo Price arena. I had expressed my reservations about the seriousness of that "sport" and he convinced me to go to the arena that evening with García Lorca to see how authentic the show really was. I talked García Lorca into it and we agreed to meet there at a certain time.[11] We were going to have great fun watching the truculence of the Masked Troglodyte, the Abyssinian Strangler, and the Sinister Orangutan.
>
> Federico did not show up. He was at that hour already on his way to death. We never saw each other again; he had an appointment with another strangler. And so the Spanish war, which changed my poetry, began for me with a poet's disappearance. (*Memoirs*, p. 122)

NOTES

1. Emir Rodríguez Monegal, *El viajero inmóvil. Introducción a Pablo Neruda* (B.A.: Losada, 1966), p. 78.
2. Federico García Lorca, "Presentacion de Pablo Neruda," in *Obras completas,* 16th ed. (Madrid: Aguilar, 1971), pp. 147-8. (Further references to this work appear parenthetically in the text as LOR)
3. Pablo Neruda, "Federico García Lorca," in *Obras completas,* 4th ed. (B.A.: Losada, 1973), III, pp. 640-1. (Further references to this work appear parenthetically in the text as NOC)
4. Neruda, *Memoirs,* trans. Hardie St. Martin (New York: Farr, Strauss and Giroux, 1977), p. 124. (Further references to this work appear parenthetically in the text)
5. Allen Josephs and Juan Caballero, "Breve panorama de la poesía lorquiana," in Lorca's *Poema del cante jondo. Romancero gitano.* (Madrid: Cátedra, 1977), p. 17
6. Neruda, *Para nacer he nacido* (Barcelona: Seiz Barral, 1978), pp. 403-4.
7. Roy Campbell, *Lorca. An Appreciation of his Poetry.* (New Haven: Yale University Press, 1952), p. 3-4.
8. Allende was assassinated on September 11, 1973, and Neruda died 12 days later, apparently from natural causes. His homes in Santiago and Valparaíso were sacked, and many of his books burned, because he had become a symbol of Marxism in Chile.
9. The complete text of this speech is available in *Memoirs,* pp. 112-3; *LOC,* pp. 145-7; and *LOC,* pp. 629-631.
10. Jorge Guillén, "Federico en persona," in *LOC,* p. LXXXI.
11. Either Neruda confused his dates, or he set this meeting with Lorca several days in advance. Lorca left Madrid for Granada on July 16.
12. Rodríguez Monegal, p. 80.
13. Carlos Morla Lynch, *En España con Federico García Lorca* (Madrid: Aguilar, 1958), p. 445.

PEGGY P. EDWARDS

LOS HUARACHES MÁGICOS

Magui Margarita Frijoles era la nieta de José Frijoles y María Paniagua de Frijoles. Vivía en Lalalandia a los pies de la Montaña de la Luz y la Montaña Oscura. Magui Margarita era lista, pero muy tímida. Sin embargo llegó a ser la líder de los niños de Lalalandia.

Tuvo un problema enorme al principio en Escuela. Cuando Maestramaestra le hacía una pregunta, se le atoraba la lengua y nomás no podía decir nada. Era tan serio su problema que los chicos se burlaban de ella.

"Magui, Magui Margarita, ¿Por qué no contestas? ¡Qué niñita más tontita! ¿Se comió el gato tu lengüita?"

Parecía que diario las cosas empeoraban. Esto, claro, preocupaba y entristecía a sus papás. Ellos recibían a diario llamadas de Maestramaestra, y hasta de la Directora, diciendo que algo se tenía que hacer. Decían,

"Cuando a Magui Margarita se le hace hasta la pregunta más fácilita, tal como, ¿Qué son dos más dos? ¿O dos por dos? Nomás no puede contestar. ¡Sabrá lo que le pasa, pero no podemos seguir así! ¡Algo se tendrá que hacer ahorita!"

Sus papás siempre se sorprendían cuando recibían estás llamadas y reportes de Escuela. Conocían muy bien a su hijita y sabían que no sólo era lista, pero era también muy sabia. A pesar de su tristeza y dolor, era buena con ellos. Se sentían de la patada. No podían imaginar cómo podían burlarse de una persona tan buena como Magui Margarita.

Sus padres ya no hallaban que hacer. Venía su cumpleaños y sólo podían pensar en su adorada hijita Magui Margarita y como mejorarle la vida. Fueron al centro comercial en busca de ese regalo que ella tanto se merecía. Entraron y salieron de muchísimas tiendas pero no encontraron nada que podía cambiarle la vida a la dulce Magui Margarita.

Después de largo rato de buscar en vano, se sentaron para descansar, cuando de repente oyeron a su lado una suave y gentil voz,

"Yo tengo lo que buscan. Yo vengo en busca de ustedes para darles este regalo para nuestra adorada Magui Margarita.'

A su lado estaba sentada una bella mujer, vestida de piel blanca; plumas azul cielo adornaban su cabello negro y sedoso. Los papás de Magui Margarita estaban asombrados. Jamás habían visto una mujer de tal sutil belleza que parecía radiar luz.

"No tengan miedo," dijo la Princesa Tolteca. "Yo vengo para ayudarles resolver su problema con su preciosa hijita. Les traigo un regalo para Magui Margarita que le cambiará la vida. Pero es para ella, y ustedes se lo deben dar al amanecer del nuevo día. Es una sorpresa especial, así que no se atrevan a abrirlo."

Luego les explicó, "Yo soy una Princesa Tolteca y vengo de un mundo raro que está muy lejos de aquí, donde no hay odio, sólo hay amor. Todos cooperan y todos nos cuidamos. No hay disputas ni batallas. Si tenemos algún problema lo resolvemos pacíficamente – platicando y escuchando con amor, paciencia y entendimiento. Todos somos iguales, pero escuchamos a nuestra gente anciana y sabia. Nuestros hijos juegan juntos y se tratan bien. No hay cárceles ni carceleros; la única ley es la justa."

Cuando terminó de hablar les entregó el regalo para Magui Margarita y a cada uno dio un beso y un abrazo. Desapareció diciendo, "Crean en mí, ténganme confianza…"

Los Frijoles fueron corriendo a casa. Tenían tentación de decirle a Magui Margarita el milagro que habían vivido, pero sabían que no podían – se lo habían prometido a la Princesa Tolteca. No dijeron ni media palabra, pero contaron las horas hasta que amaneciera su día especial.

Cuando el quiquiriquí de su gallo anunció el amanecer de ese día esplendido, los tres Frijoles ya estaban parados y alertas. Magui Margarita, la primera en levantarse, sospechó que este sería un día espectacular. Naturalmente, lo primero que le dieron a Magui Margarita fue su misterioso regalo de la Princesa Tolteca. Pero primero le contaron la historia de la mística Princesa Tolteca de un mundo lejano.

Magui Margarita entonces, ansiosa pero cuidadosa, abrió su regalo. Dentro del paquete encontró un par de huaraches blancos, bordados con cuentas y plumas azul cielo -- eran preciosos. Se los puso inmediatamente y, no cabe decir que le quedaron como guante.

El siguiente día en Escuela, Magui Margarita se veía fabulosa con sus huaraches nuevos. Los chicos pronto se dieron cuenta que ella ya no era la misma Magui Margarita tímida que casi ni abría la boca.

Cuando Maestramaestra le hacía cualquier pregunta, ahora ella contestaba correctamente y con lujo de detalle. Explicaba tan bien sus respuestas que hasta parecía maestra. Ya no se le atoraba la lengua – podía hablar fluidamente. De hecho sus palabras le salían como seda. Pronto los niños se dieron cuenta que Magui Margarita era muy sabia y comenzaron a pedirle consejos.

Chicharito, que le encantaba jugar fútbol, se moría por jugar fútbol en el equipo Escuela. Dijo, "Es lo que más quiero, pero ellos no me van a querer porque soy flaquito, chiquito, y no juego tan bien como ellos."

Magui Margarita le aconsejó, "La actitud lo es todo. Cambia tu manera de pensar. Haz un plan. Práctica todos los días. Apréndete las mejores jugadas. Acércate a ello y velos jugar. Demuéstrales que lo puedes hacer. Y sobre todo no tengas miedo. No tardarás en aprender bien. Sé paciente. Aprende a jugar en equipo. Verás que pronto todos te van a querer en su equipo."

Chicharito siguió los consejos de Magui Margarita y hoy día es un jugador de fútbol famosísimo. Susiquiu también le pidió consejo (se quejó que nadie la quería).

"Eso no es cierto," dijo Magui Margarita, "Yo te quiero y sé que muchos otros cuates también te quieren. Sé buena amiga. No seas negativa o vengativa. Sé amigable y escucha a tus amigos con cuidado. Sé positiva." Susiquiu siguió sus consejos y hoy es una chica muy bien querida.

La vida de Magui Margarita dio un gran giro, y cuando pensaba que todo le iba de maravilla, lo predecible ocurrió. Una tormenta explotó sobre la tierra, y en esa tormenta se le empaparon sus huaraches mágicos.

¿Qué haría? No los podía usar así a Escuela. Lo pensó largo rato y con mucho cuidado. Su primer impulso era quedarse en casa ese día. ¿Qué importaba si se quedaba en casa por sólo un día? Pero entonces pensó, *eso no es nada responsable y muy cobarde. Yo que doy los mejores consejos no puedo ser la que no puede. Pues bien, iré, y pase lo que pase, que será será.*

Así que (un poco temerosa), se puso unos zapatos cualquiera y se fue a Escuela. Nadie ni se fijó que Magui Margarita no usaba sus maravillosos huaraches mágicos. Como siempre, Maestramaestra le hizo las preguntas más difíciles.

Se le comenzaba a trabar la lengua y tartamudeó al principio. Pero luego se acordó de todo lo bueno que había hecho, y suave como la seda, las respuestas perfectas fluían de su boca.

Después de eso Magui Margarita le aconsejó a Juanita Julia, que estaba deprimida tocante a su situación, y ya no podía concentrarse. Dijo,
"Mi Mamita ya no me quiere. Tengo un hermanito nuevo, y ya a mí sólo me pone atención cuando me porto mal."
Magui Margarita le aconsejó que ayudara a su Mamita en todo lo que podía. Dijo que su hermanito era un regalo muy especial para toda la familia. Le dijo,
"El miedo, odio, y malos pensamientos se pueden parar. Tienes que pensar positivamente. Ama, confía, ayuda y escucha. Mantente enfocada. Esas son las cosas que sí puedes y debes hacer. Acuérdate que sólo tú puedes mejorar tu vida. Siempre escoge hacer cosas buenas, porque al fin de cuentas, esas siempre te van a salir bien hechas. Y si después de hacer todo lo que te digo, aun necesitas los huaraches mágicos, pídemelos para que te los preste."
Algún día, si tienes suerte tú también vas a conocer a Magui Margarita. Ella a menudo escala la Montaña de la Luz para visitar a sus abuelos los Frijoles.
De allí puede mirar a toda Lalalandia.
Y colorín, colorado, este cuento se ha acabado.

THE MAGIC MOCCASINS

Maggie Margaret Beans was the granddaughter of Joe beans and Mary Breadnwater. She lived in Lalaland at the foot of the Mountain of Light and the Dark Mountain. Maggie Margaret was smart, but very shy. Nevertheless she became the leader of the children of Lalaland.

At first she had an enormous problem at School. When Teacherteacher asked her a question her tongue got stuck and she couldn't say a thing. Her problem was so bad that the kids made fun of her,

"Maggie, Maggie Margaret, why don't you answer? Such a big dummy! Did the cat eat your tongue-y?"

Daily, it seemed, things got worse. This, of course, worried and saddened her parents. They got daily calls from Teacherteacher and even from the Principal, saying something had to be done. They said,

"When Maggie Margaret is asked even the easiest question, such as, what is two plus two? Or two times two?' She just can't answer. Who knows what's wrong with her, but we can't go on like this. Something must be done now!"

Her parents were always surprised when they received these school calls and reports. They knew their daughter very well and they knew she was not only smart, but also very wise. In spite of her sadness and pain, she was good to them. They felt terrible. They couldn't imagine how anyone could make fun of such a good person as Maggie Margaret.

Her parents were beside themselves. Her birthday was close and they could only think about their adorable child and how to improve her life. They went to the shopping mall in search of that gift she so much deserved. They entered and exited many stores but could not find that gift that could change the life of their sweet Maggie Margaret.

After looking for a long time in vain, they sat down to rest, when suddenly they heard beside them a soft and gentle voice,

"I have what you are in search of. I have been looking for you to give you a gift for our adored Maggie Margaret."

Beside them sat a lovely woman, dressed in white leather; sky-blue feathers adorned her black-silky hair. Maggie Margaret's parents were amazed. They had never seen a woman of such subtle beauty that she seemed to radiate light.

"Do not be afraid," said the Toltec Princess. "I come to help you solve this problem with your precious daughter. I bring you a gift for Maggie Margaret which will change her life. But it's for her, and you should give it to her at the dawning of the new day. It's a special surprise, so don't you dare open it."

She went on to explain, "I am a Toltec Princess and I come from a strange-faraway world where there is no hate, only love. Everyone cooperates and we all take care of one another. There are no fights or battles. If we have a problem we take care of it peacefully – speaking and listening with love, patience and understanding. We are all equals, but we listen to our elders who are wise. Our children play together and get along. There are no jails or jailers; the only law is fair."

When she finished talking she gave them the gift for Maggie Margaret and to each gave a kiss and a hug. She disappeared saying, "Believe in me, have faith in me…"

The Beans went running home. They were tempted to tell Maggie Margaret the miracle they had lived, but they knew they couldn't – they had promised the Toltec Princess. They didn't utter a word, but they counted the hours her special day would dawn.

When the cock-a-doodle-doo of their rooster announced the dawning of that splendid day, the three Beans were already up and alert. Maggie Margaret, the first to get up, suspected that this would be a spectacular day. Naturally, the first thing they gave Maggie Margaret was her mysterious gift from the Toltec Princess. But first they told her the mystic Toltec Princess' story who came from a faraway land.

Maggie Margaret then, anxiously, but carefully opened her gift. Within the package she found a pair of white moccasins, embroidered with precious stones and sky-blue feathers – they were beautiful. She put them on immediately and, needless to say, they fit her like a glove.

The following day Maggie Margaret looked fabulous in her new moccasins. The kids soon realized she was not the same old timid Maggie Margaret who hardly dared to open her mouth.

When Teacherteacher asked her any question, now she answered correctly and with details. She explained her answers so well that she even seemed to be the teacher. Her tongue no longer got stuck in her mouth – she could speak fluently. In fact her words flowed out like silk. The kids soon realized Maggie Margaret was very wise and they began to ask her for advice.

Sweetpea, who loved to play soccer, was dying to play on School's team. He said,

"That's what I want most, but they won't want me because I'm skinny, small, and don't play as well as them."

Maggie Margaret advised him, "Attitude is everything. Change how you think. Make a plan. Practice every day. Learn the best plays. Get close to them and watch them play. Show them you can do it. Above all don't be afraid. It won't take you long to learn well. Be patient. Learn to play on a team. You'll see that soon they'll want you on their team."

Sweetpea followed Maggie Margaret's advice and today he is a very famous soccer player. Susyq also asked for advice, she complained nobody loved her.

"That's not true," said Maggie Margaret. "I love you and I know lots of others who do too. Be a good friend. Don't be negative or vindictive. Be friendly and listen to your friends carefully. Be positive." Susyq followed her advice and today she is very-well liked.

Maggie Margaret's life improved a great deal, and when she thought things couldn't get better, the predictable happened. A storm exploded on earth, that storm soaked her magic moccasins.

What could she do? She couldn't wear them like that to School. She thought about it for a long time and very carefully. Her first impulse was to stay home that day. What did it matter if she only missed one day? But then she thought, *that's not responsible and very cowardly. I, who give the best advice can't be the one who can't. Well fine, I'll go, and whatever will be, will be.*

So (a little bit afraid), she put on any old shoes and went to School. No one even noticed that Maggie Margaret was not wearing her marvelous magic moccasins. As always, Teacherteacher asked her the most difficult questions.

Her tongue almost got stuck and she stuttered at first. But then she remembered all the good she did, and soft as silk, perfect answers flowed from her mouth.

After that Maggie Margaret advised Joanie Jean who was so depressed she could no longer concentrate. She said,

125

"My Mommy doesn't love me anymore. I have a new brother, and she only pays attention to me when I misbehave."

Maggie Margaret advised her to help her Mommy in every way she could. She said her brother was a very special gift for the whole family. She said,

"Fear, hate, bad thoughts can be stopped. You have to think positively. Love, have faith, help and listen. Stay focused. Those are all things you can do. Remember only you can improve your life. Always choose good things to do, because, after all, those always turn out right. And if after you do all that I say, and you still need the magic moccasins, ask me for them and I'll lend them to you."

Some day, if you're lucky, you too will meet Maggie Margaret. She often climbs the Mountain of light to visit her grandparents, the Beans.

From there she can see all of Lalaland.

POETRY

JULIA BLOEMEKE

OBSERVATIONS FROM THE BASE

Lake Santeetlah, North Carolina
The problem with heights:
They are heights.
Again the resistance
of water.
How each kiss, somehow,
is an attempt to recreate,
not make new.
Lust: a four-letter word.
Also: what.
I have self-covenants:
One: to imagine no
other when with you.
By the fire, I slip.
I curse myself
for not loving better.
When I ask you if I am
someone else you say,
Only you.
I want to be this mountain.
But then I swim.
The problem with covenants:
They are covenants.
Later you say this to me:
The blank space is how
I honor it, deliciously gone.
Even the fog makes promises,
spans the hips of mountains.
Such great heights.
The fire wet ashes
we cannot light again.

RICK HILL

THE LITTLE DEIST

*The Hummingbird (*Mellisuga Minimas*) has a longer lifespan
potential than other organisms with such a high metabolism. The
Alpha male is typically very territorial. Once he finds an artificial
feeder, he will fight off smaller hummingbirds to maintain complete
dominance over the sugar source. Most hummingbirds of the U.S.
and Canada migrate south in fall to southern Mexico or Central
America.*

—Wikipedia

Judy boiled the sugar down, four scoops to one part water
Strained the cloudy sauce into her *Mellisuga* feeder
Hung a prudent distance from the ancient seed dispenser
With its cracked ceramic figures of Saint Francis and his flock.

Four yellow bakelite daisies where the smaller fry may suckle
Four faux-vine plastic perches here to rest upon while supping
"Come make yourself at home, boys, and calm your restless flapping
Enjoy our graceland patio, our port from tooth and claw!"

Minimas came swooping in, a dozen up the canyon
Chittering like cellophane on after-dinner stogies
Sipping in rotation as the wind chimes jingled softly
Wasps and monarchs flutter by; said Judy, "It's all good."

But all too soon concupiscence gave way to darker patterns:
a jumbo hummist, longer beak, loud chit and greener feathers
Declared a no-fly zone out to the Easter Lily cactus
Proclaimed the feeder his domain and drove the rest away.

All summer long he fights them off and chitters imprecations
The mating dance abandoned, likewise honeysuckle blossoms
He's tethered to his treasure cache, his fount of gall and wormwood
From her kitchen window Judy ponders what will come.

Will this tiny bon vivant go gummy-beaked and paunchy?
Can his potential lifespan gel in such frenetic tension?

Will wasps lay brazen larvae in his delicate chest feathers
When hubris hits the concrete slab with frenzied heartbeat stilled?

Judy cries, "What have we wrought?" and doubts her inclinations
"How can we judge? How dared we set this sad machine in motion?
If we take his burden he'll forsake our yard and curse us
We must not intervene for we have interfered enough."

Inside it's warm as autumn chills the patio deserted
Judy sips hot cider while she surfs the nature channels
Eleven seekers humming south to Costa Rican jungles
One ruminates upon his perch and formulates this myth.

SADIQULLAH KHAN

AGONIZING OVER POETRY

Whose word, whose song —
Tu Fu was "agonizing over poetry"
Under a straw hat, exhausted and sad.
When Li Po met him atop a hill.
'Your words were either a consolation,'
The Bard said, 'life was an insignificant story,
Told by an idiot.'
I read the verse again and again.
The unseen rain a hailstorm of stones,
And weaving winds turned to storms,
What a balmy glance, what a touch —
Lo! Your beauty can raise the anguished heart.

LISA LUNNEY

INNOCENCE OF NATURE

The great moments of life are often the mundane.
The feel of warm summer air after a hard winter.
Birdsong in a wooded wonderland.

The greatest moments in life.
We neglect.
We ignore.

These great moments.
The treasures we neglect.
We forget.

It seems like a vivid dream.
At best.

Time passes.
All you have left is this tiny.
Crisp. fragment.

You no longer remember what happened.
It's more of an idea what happened.

The innocence and beauty of nature.
Is always the most cherished memory.
That we neglect.

ROBBI NESTER

LOOKING AT JUPITER

After Mary Boxley Bullington's painting "Reinventing the Color Wheel"

In a kaleidoscope, shards of colored glass
drop into slots on a segmented wheel.
Red petals fall from a rose,
leaves from a tree,
then reattach.
When I turn to the window,
a red house appears, its pointed roof
tipped with flame.
A rainy afternoon offers umbrellas,
patterned like the underside of a frond
with unreadable braille.

We used to think space was empty,
full of dead rock, dark matter,
but here is Jupiter, tossing her orange scarves,
67 moons whirling around her
in orbits more intricate
than any Hollywood choreographer
could devise.
Ice matched with fire,
every hue that ever was.
Much depends on the flick of a wrist,
the position of the observer,
the play of light on clouds.

JOHN ROULEAU

POETIC SUITE

Haiku
spring wraps the plum tree
in a pink kimono of
delicate blossoms
•

An unopened bud
A promise
Of future beauty
•

december branches
sleep deep in winter's blanket
dreaming of spring
•

i hear you breathing
beneath your cold white blanket
earth, quiet, resting

For My Daughter Ming Ming
She knows I'm leaving
by the jangling of my keys.
"Bye daddy! Love you!"
•

Will we always
be so close, daughter?
•

You will always
have a mansion
in my heart.

Ridiculous
At least
I'm being ridiculous
In the privacy
Of my
Own home.
In the dark.
Doors closed.
Blinds drawn.
Only myself
To mock me.
Only myself
To blame.

Rare
pausing to watch
a rare snowfall
each flake unique
as each of us each
reflecting white
light on a grey day between
me and a blue pine

Daybreak
Sunday solitude
at daybreak.
At this sacred window
I stand, hoping
rain will wash
away our sins, wondering
if sad souls
are reborn
as mourning doves.

Amber
In the cold
dark of winter
an amber lamp
on the counter
in my kitchen
glows.
And by
its warm
and gentle light
a tiny plant
in a corner 'neath
the cupboard
grows.

For MLK Jr.
January 18th
Martin Luther King Junior Day, again.
Forty-nine years since
you stood
alone
on that fateful balcony.
•
I open the kitchen window
to smell fresh rain,
to hear the wind
in the winter garden,
to think of you, Martin.
Still
gone, still
not quiet.
•
This old world
keeps on
turning, ever lonely
in a
dark corner
of space. We,

still prone
to turning
out the light.

You
You
are not
a collectible.
You are
rare,
fine,
one of a kind.
And I hope
that you
believe it,
Too.

Japan. Rain.
Japanese countryside.
Rainy Day. In cool mist
puddle ducks paddle
downstream and up
nibbling fresh
green shoots.
Perfection.
On the train
a respectful
Silence.

J. MATTHEW WATERS

going underground

ants are everywhere
and most of them are downright
industrious

then there's the spiders
and snakes and whatever nature
wants to sally forth populating this place

ground squirrels moved in
last week
little sons a bitches

neighbor says he's got a
groundhog
living up there
behind them bushes

wolves and foxes make for
scary noises
beyond the border trees at night

or maybe it's just two cats without gloves
settling an old match
or better yet
an adolescent sasquatch
out looking for a snack

beneath all the commotion
subhumans thrive at
twenty-four seven bizarres
peddling flashlights and canteens
and cuban cigars
dark chocolate squares
and high powered rifles

ROBERT YEHLING

WITH SOMETHING OF ANGELIC LIGHT

(Echo from a William Wordsworth line…)

With something of angelic light
she glides through the world,
her touch present on smiles
of the homeless & struggling
as they press on,
conversing with their own angels,
pieces of themselves
left behind in silent furies and alleys
trying to make ends meet
before the ends stopped meeting
and became bitter rivals
determined to outmaneuver the other —

so the story in the head goes —

Then the conversation turns
And all becomes okay
Because flowers, when you look closely,
Smile back from the eyes of angels
And that is what we can see
Whether carrying all that's left
On our backs
Or connecting those two ends again
And soaring within ourselves
With something of angelic light.

ROBERT YEHLING

TOMORROW KNOWS

Pulling
      us toward
           new tomorrows

The wind,
caught in its story
of how it carried
a seed far from native ground
and deposited it into a canyon

Where, years later,
we walked underneath palms
into streamside grass
and emerged with you,
our child.

Where your
      seed grows,
           tomorrow knows.

OUR CONTRIBUTORS

JULIE BLOEMEKE is a writer and poet on the rise. Her first collection, *Slide to Unlock,* was a finalist for the 2016 May Swenson Poetry Award through the University Press of Colorado and Utah State University Press. *Slide to Unlock* was a semifinalist in six other competitions nationwide. She has been published in more than 20 literary journals, including *Crab Orchard Revise, Muse/A Journal, Chautauqua Literary Journal,* and *The Great Gatsby Anthology.* She is the current creative writing fellow at the University of Virginia. You can view more of her work at *www.jebloemeke.com.*

PEGGY P. EDWARDS Born and raised in Mexico City, Edwards came to the United States to complete her education. She received her BA from Southern Methodist University and her MA from the University of Wisconsin. She taught university, college, ESL, high school, elementary, and preschool – always focusing on Spanish and English. She is retired in Laguna Woods Village, CA. She is president of the Village Publishing Club. She published "Alfabeto Crossover Alphabet" and "Lalalandia" – eight bilingual, mystical stories of a land saved by music. *villagepublishingclub.com.*

MARTÍN ESPADA was a 2007 Pulitzer Prize finalist for his collection, *The Republic of Poetry.* He has written 13 poetry collections and three books of essays, including *The Lover of a Subversive Is Also a Subversive.* He is one of the most celebrated poets in the Western Hemisphere, and the recipient of the National Endowment for the Arts Creative Writing Fellowship, Pushcart Prize, Robert Creeley Award, Guggenheim Fellowship, Paterson Award for Sustained Literary Achievement, and 2012 International Latino Book Award. A poetry professor at the University of Massachusetts, Martin has appeared many times in *The Hummingbird Review.*

ROBERT L. GLEAVES was a literary and academic writer. "Neruda & Lorca: A Meeting of Poetic Minds", reprinted and featured in this issue, first appeared in 1980 in *Research Studies,* University of North Carolina at Charlotte. It also appeared in 1997 in *Confluencia,* published by the University of Northern Colorado.

RICK HILL, an Iowa Writers Workshop graduate, directs the Writing major at Point Loma Nazarene University. Publications include poems, stories, and essays in numerous journals and books on Mark Twain and C.S. Lewis. His childhood memoir *We're All From Somewhere Else* (a San Diego Book Award winner) is available on Amazon.com.

SADIQULLAH KHAN is a prolific writer of contemporary, socially conscious poetry, drawing inspiration from the literary traditions of his native Pakistan. He is the author of *The Voices, Chaos of Being,* and *The Songs of Other Times.* A resident of Islamabad, he previously appeared in the Fall/Winter 2015 issue of *The Hummingbird Review.*

ISAAC LOMELI is an author, teacher, essayist, and championship wrestling coach. A lifelong Southern Californian, he has written about the Latino experience in bridging two cultures for the past ten years. His own experience forms the basis: he avoided street gangs as a youth by turning to literature to find meaning and purpose in his life. He has completed two books: *Tales from the Eastside,* a memoir previewed in the Winter/Spring 2011 issue of *The Hummingbird Review;* and *The Unexamined Life of a Brown Man,* excerpted in this issue. He lives in Anaheim, CA.

LISA LUNNEY spends her days working as a freelance writer, but she also is a fine poet. A journalist, essayist and poet based in Calgary, Alberta, Lisa has written for a number of U.S. and Canadian publications and journals. She previously appeared in the Fall/Winter 2015 issue of *The Hummingbird Review.*

LYDIA MASCARIN was born in Los Angeles of Mexican-American heritage. She has fed her passion for nature and art all of her life. She dabbles in sculpture, painting, poetry and music. She now resides in Laguna Woods Village, enjoying the numerous natural gifts of southern California.

ELLYN MAYBE, Southern California based poet, United States Artist nominee 2012, has performed both nationally and internationally as a solo artist and with her band. Her work has been included in many anthologies and she is the author of numerous books. She also has a critically acclaimed poetry/music album, *Rodeo for the Sheepish* (Hen House Studios). In addition to her

band, her latest poetry/music project is called ellyn & robbie. Their new album is called *Skywriting with Glitter.*
ellynmaybe.com
ellynandrobbie.com

DEAN NELSON is the founder and host of the annual Writer's Symposium by the Sea at Point Loma Nazarene University in San Diego, the program at which former Poet Laureate of the United States Robert Pinsky appeared. Others who have spoken include Billy Collins, the late Ray Bradbury, the late George Plimpton, Kathleen Norris, Bill Moyers, Joseph Wambaugh, and many others. A long-time professor at PLNU, Dean is the author or co-author of 12 books, including *God Hides in Plain Sight: How to Find the Sacred in a Chaotic World.* He is a contributor to the *New York Times, Boston Globe, Christianity Today, Sojourners,* and others. His work previously appeared in the Spring/Summer 2013 issue of *The Hummingbird Review.*

ROBBI NESTER lives and writes in Southern California. She is the author of an ekphrastic chapbook, Balance (White Violet, 2012) and a collection of poems, A Likely Story (Moon Tide, 2014), and has edited two anthologies, The Liberal Media Made Me Do It! (Nine Toes, 2014) and Over the Moon: Birds, Beasts, and Trees-- celebrating the photography of Beth Moon. Her poetry, essays, reviews, articles, etc. have appeared in many journals, anthologies, websites, and web blogs.

CHARLES REDNER is the founder and publisher of *The Hummingbird Review* and author of five books, including *Down But Never Out* and *Terror Travels the Devil's Highway.*

JOHN ROULEAU adds to his stature as the only contributor who has appeared in every issue of *The Hummingbird Review.* His haiku, short verse, and vignettes have delighted our readers for both their incisiveness and the storytelling within. Raised on the banks of the St. Croix River bordering Wisconsin and Minnesota, where his attunement to nature formed, he now lives, writes, and paints in the hills of the East Bay near San Francisco.

LUIS ALBERTO URREA is the inspiration behind *The Hummingbird Review,* as his conversations with Charles Redner in 2007 and 2008, and early involvement, led to the creation of the anthology. A member of the Latin Literature Hall of Fame, winner of dozens of awards, and the critically-acclaimed author of 16 books, including *Into the Beautiful North,* excerpted in this issue. Luis was a 2005 Pulitzer Prize Finalist for Nonfiction for *The Devil's Highway.* His most recent book, *Water Music,* was a 2015 book of the year in *The Washington Post* and *Kirkus Review,* and a finalist for the PEN-Faulkner Award. More than 100 cities have chosen his books for One-Book Community Read programs. He lives in Naperville, Illinois, where he is a distinguished professor of creative writing at the University of Illinois-Chicago.

J. MATTHEW WATERS is author of the poetry collection, *In the Middle of Somewhere,* available on amazon.com. His colorful poems interweave inner perception and outer observation using nature as the structural framework. He previously appeared in the Fall/Winter 2015 issue of *The Hummingbird Review.* He is based in Cedar Rapids, Iowa.

ROBERT YEHLING is the Editor of *The Hummingbird Review* and the author or co-author of 20 books, including the novel *Voices* and five poetry collections, most recently *Backroad Melodies.* He lives in Southern California. His books are available on amazon.com, and other works are on *www.wordjourneysliterary.com.*

YOUR *HUMMINGBIRD REVIEW* COLLECTION

Just learning about *The Hummingbird Review?* Have you missed a couple of issues over the years? Want to own the entire collection? A look at the previous six issues of *The Hummingbird Review*, and some of the authors, poets, essayists, journalists, memoirists and songwriters who contributed and/or were featured:

Back copies are available at:
Amazon.com/books/the hummingbird review or at
amazon.com/books/charles redner

VOL. 1, NO. 1: Winter/Spring 2010
Interviews:
Filmmaker ERNESTO LIVON-GROSSMAN
Poet TAYLOR MALI
Featured Works:
LUIS ALBERTO URREA • MARTÍN ESPADA • TAYLOR MALI • ELIA
ESPARZA • CHARLES REDNER • KATHRYN KOPPLE • ROBERT
WRIGLEY • CARLOS CUMPIAN

VOL. 1, NO. 2: Summer/Fall, 2010
Interview:
Memoirist PATRICIA VOLONAKIS DAVIS
Featured Works:
MICHAEL SHRIEVE/Santana • SAM SHRIEVE • LUIS ALBERTO URREA
• MICHAEL BLAKE • VALARIE JAMES • DEAN NELSON • MAGGI
DEROSA • DON EULERT • BILL MAWHINNEY • SAID LEGHLID

VOL. 2, NO. 1: Spring/Summer 2011
Interviews:
Pulitzer Prize-winning poet GARY SNYDER
Broadway Composer DAVID AMRAM
Featured Work:
JOY HARJO • MICHAEL BLAKE • HARVEY STANBROUGH • GARY
LAWLESS • WILLIAM THOMPSON ONG • RYKA AOKI • ISAAC LOMELI
• KATE HARDING • THEA IBERALL • DICK EIDEN • ROBERT YEHLING
• HARRY GRISWOLD

VOL. 3, NO. 1: Spring/Summer 2012
Interview:
Author NOAM CHOMSKY
Featured Work:
BRIAN WILKES • JOHN GARDINER • ADAM RODMAN • CHERYL
MERRILL • FARZANA VERSEY • CHARLES REDNER • THEA IBERALL
• TJ DEMA • BATSARAI E. CHIGAMA

VOL. 4, NO. 1: Spring/Summer 2013
Interview:
Poet Laureate of the United States BILLY COLLINS
Featured Work:
DEAN NELSON • MICHAEL BLAKE • MANNY PACHECO • JOHN DOE
• STEVIE SALAS • MARTIN ESPADA • ERICA GOSS • BILL STUDEBAKER
• GAIL BORNFIELD • RICKI MANDEVILLE • JOHN GARDINER
• ROXANNE PILAT • KATHRYN KOPPLE

VOL. 5, NO. 1: Winter/Spring 2016
Interviews:
Fictionist/poet E.E. KING
Featured Work:
E.E. KING • MICHAEL C. FORD • MICHAEL BLAKE • WILLIAM
THOMPSON ONG • ROBERT YEHLING • GLORIA CREED-DIKEOGU
• SADIQULLAH KHAN • WILLIAM LANGTRY • ROBIN HUDECHEK
• LISA LUNNEY • AMY MOSHER • MICHAEL SCHOFIELD

www.ingramcontent.com/pod-product-compliance
Lightning Source LLC
Chambersburg PA
CBHW071346170626
46811CB00003B/1006